CANCELLED

TED BUNDY
America's Most Evil Serial Killer

Al Cimino

PICTURE CREDITS

Topfoto: 8, 72, 168, 172

Shutterstock: 15, 74

Getty Images: 16, 36, 67, 125, 154, 162, 165, 177, 181, 197

Shutterstock editorial: 57, 110, 113, 114, 179, 189, 250, 251

This edition published in 2019 by Arcturus Publishing Limited
26/27 Bickels Yard, 151–153 Bermondsey Street,
London SE1 3HA

AD006674UK

Printed in the UK

TED BUNDY

Contents

All-American Boy

TED BUNDY was a prolific rapist and murderer who assaulted and killed as many as 36 women and girls. His acts were horrifically degenerate and depraved. But his family and friends had no inkling of what he was up to. His lovers were unaware – or when they did harbour suspicions they were easily persuaded to put them out of mind. On the face of it, Bundy did not look like anyone's idea of a killer.

When he finally went on trial for the murder of two college students in Florida and the brutal assault of three others, *The New York Times* said: 'The stereotype of mass killers – with minds bedeviled by tumors or hallucinations – is all too familiar to the American republic. They were the drifters, the malcontents, the failures and the resenters. Ted Bundy, for all appearances, no way resembles any of them. He had all the personal resources that are prized in America, that guarantee success and respect.

He loved children, read poetry, showed courage by chasing down and capturing a purse-snatcher on the streets of Seattle, rescued a child from drowning, loved the outdoors, respected his parents, was a college honors student, worked with desperate people at a crisis center and, in the words of one admirer, "Ted could be with any woman he wanted – he was so magnetic!" He wanted to become an attorney or a politician, to do something with his life to help others.'

By then Bundy had already been convicted of aggravated kidnapping in Utah, yet *The New York Times* headline read: 'All-American boy on trial'. He was charming, handsome and charismatic. No one believed that he could have done it.

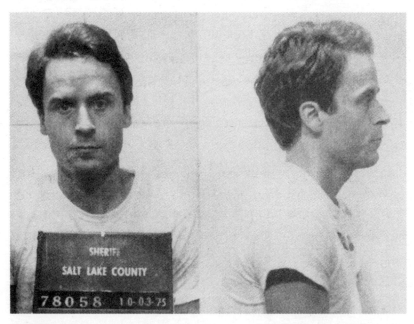

Ted Bundy looked like he had it all – he seemed like the perfect All-American boy – but appearances can be deceptive.

'For God's sake,' said a man who knew the young Ted Bundy before his first criminal charges, 'he was so well thought of that he was the assistant director of the Seattle Crime Prevention Advisory Commission the same year all the killings started.' In that office, Bundy even wrote a rape prevention pamphlet. Meanwhile, he was a Republican campaigner staffer and a rising star in the GOP.

Almost to the end, there were a lot of people who believed that Bundy himself was the victim – a bright young man tangled in a monstrous web of circumstance by a jealous girlfriend and persecuted by conniving police investigators, ambitious prosecutors and lazy journalists, who were happy to pile one charge on top of another, making the case bigger and more sensational. However, in his final days, when Bundy eventually faced the electric chair after years on Death Row, he confessed to a litany of unspeakable crimes. His wife, who had married him when he was already under sentence of death and had stuck by him through thick and thin, was shocked and distraught, and disappeared with their child.

Although Bundy had been on the list of suspects for murders in Washington State, Idaho, Utah, Colorado and Florida, the police could not catch him and doctors did not diagnose his psychopathic condition until it was way too late. Even then they were hard put to explain why he had committed his appalling crimes.

As a child he was shy, but not unusually so. His first girlfriend found him immature, but sensed nothing of the violent sexual fantasies that were already gripping him. Seven years later, she met a now grown-up Ted Bundy and tried to rekindle their relationship, unaware that he was already a practised peeping tom and stalker.

Odd coincidences led his long-term girlfriend Liz Kendall to have her suspicions, but she castigated herself for talking to the police, fearing she might ruin his political career. The police, in turn, dismissed her misgivings, seeing Bundy as a blameless law student with no criminal record – not the sort of man who raped, sodomized and murdered. Liz found it hard to believe that a man who was accused of having just sated his perverted lust with brutal murder could be sitting across the dinner table from her, talking like a normal human being. She finally split from him, but still called her book about their time together *The Phantom Prince*, betraying more than a little affection for the demented serial killer.

A co-worker at a counselling centre where Bundy worked was a former police officer and crime writer. She even accepted a commission to write a book about the killings that were gripping Washington State in 1974, without realizing that the man who had occupied the adjacent desk was responsible. Even when the truth came out, she found it hard to credit.

Carole Ann Boone, the woman who became his wife, dismissed his multiple convictions until, she said, she saw irrefutable physical evidence. Even that was not good enough. When the authorities forbade their marriage she found a way to do it anyway – and give him a child while he was on Death Row.

Then there were the groupies who turned up at Bundy's trial. They wrote to him begging for his love.

Liz Kendall in the embrace of her long-term lover Ted Bundy; Kendall was conflicted over her attempts to turn Bundy in. He had that effect on many people; they simply couldn't believe he could be bad.

His victims were similarly susceptible. They would be taken in by his winning smile and volunteered to lend a hand when he asked for help, before discovering that his apparent helplessness was merely a ruse. By then it was too late and they suffered the most horrifying deaths, their bodies further defiled afterwards.

Having worked on the Crime Prevention Advisory Commission in Washington State, Bundy knew how the police operated so he spread his murders through various jurisdictions, making it hard for the authorities to co-ordinate their investigations. It was not clear, to start with, that all the murders were the work of one man.

Indeed, the police were helpless to stop him. They did not track him down. Nor did they solve the various cases. Bundy was brought down by hubris, drawing attention to himself as if believing that he could not be captured. Picked up for minor offences, he foolishly invited investigation for weightier matters. Even when charged with kidnapping, attempted murder and murder itself, he might well have got away with it had he not chosen to represent himself in court. Professional legal counsel might well have got him off. He even escaped from jail – not once, but twice – when facing a capital charge.

As to understanding his motivation, Bundy was as much in the dark as the psychologists and psychiatrists who examined him. Only at the very end did he admit, even to himself, what he was really capable of.

By then he had had enough time to study the workings of serial killers, both by extensive reading and rubbing shoulders with other mass murderers in jail. He got to know his subject so well that he worked with one of the detectives who had pursued him in the investigation of a new serial killer who was then plaguing Washington State.

The detective concerned was Robert 'Bob' Keppel, by this time Chief Criminal Investigator for the Washington State Attorney General, who wrote a book about his collaboration with Bundy called *The Riverman* – Bundy's name for the serial killer more commonly known as the Green River Killer, Gary Ridgway. He, like Bundy, would strangle his victims and dump their bodies in a remote area so he could return to have sex with the corpse, if it had not been discovered.

Ridgway was not arrested until more than ten years after Bundy was dead. But their collaboration gave Keppel a profound insight into Bundy's psyche. He wrote: 'Even though every murderer is different in nature, Bundy shared certain characteristics with other serial killers. Ted was a loner. Inside, he was extremely insecure. While striving for security, he made life miserable for the rest of us. His relationships with others were very superficial. He was a fellow who could not stick with anyone. His relatives and acquaintances may have tried very hard to have contact with him, thus feeling that they were very close to him. Many of his friends, both old and new, were starved for love and affection. They felt what Ted wanted them to feel because he was able to detect and exploit people's needs. In a way, he made victims of all who knew him.'

Keppel noted that what added to Ted's convincing nature was that he was intelligent, attractive and charming – traits that most of his admirers found pleasing. His reputation was that of an aspiring lawyer and a bright young man who was dutiful to family.

'But when Ted murmured gratitude, his words came from an empty heart,' Keppel said. 'He would cast off friends without a thought, and once alienated, he could reel them back in like bloated trout. There was always something about Ted that they liked and kept coming back to. His efforts to maintain friendships were nothing more than attempts to preserve control over those very people he used for his own purposes.'

Keppel found that Bundy was an almost complete sociopath who made no distinction between what he wanted and what belonged to someone else. He had absolutely no sense of boundaries and sought to exercise his control over anyone who crossed his path.

'Because of Ted's appearance of having a winning, good-guy bravado, his friends thought that he was the last person who would have murdered anyone,' Keppel said. 'Over the years, anytime I saw news stories in which friends of a suspected killer said, "He was such a nice boy, he couldn't have done it," I thought of Ted and said to myself that the police had the right guy.'

Keppel concluded that Bundy did not just have a split personality, but there were four Bundys hiding behind one mask.

'At first, it was as if Ted were the Riverman himself, the cunning psychopath, planning and practicing the lures he used with women, familiarizing himself with appropriate dump sites, checking his routes to and from, and meticulously planning what he would do after the murder to cover his tracks. He projected that personality during our interviews.

'The second was an almost hapless version of Ted, the disorganized neurotic, a loser often in a drunken stupor, a frightened, reluctant killer traumatized by his murderous behaviour, and afraid of having any remembrance of his most recent murder anywhere near him. It wasn't that he was afraid of getting caught; he was afraid his neurotic personality would completely disintegrate in front of whomever he was with, and he would do anything to get it away from him. His neurotic tendencies also drew unnecessary attention to him. That neurosis allowed Bundy to give too much information about himself to potential victims that he did not abduct.

'The third Ted that I observed was the self-serving, swashbuckling, hypergrandiose paranoid, driven by an eerie bravado and dazzled by his own sense of omnipotence,

Investigator Bob Keppel concluded that Bundy did not just have a split personality; there were four Bundys hiding behind one mask.

who personally negotiated with governors and attorneys general, and held beleaguered relatives of murder victims and detectives hostage with information. That third Ted behaved like a cruel despot, indifferent to the reality that was taking place around him. Ted's grandiose behaviour was exemplified best by his own words, spoken to me after he finished confessing and was ready to negotiate for his life on the Friday prior to his Tuesday execution.'

But in the end there was the fourth Ted Bundy, the tearful man who did not want to die, who bargained the details of each

Who was this man? And why did he like attention so much? Ted Bundy acting up in a Miami courtroom after the judge had left the room.

murder and his knowledge of where the bodies were dumped, which might have brought some closure to the families of victims, for another few days to live. He went to the electric chair in 1989.

The story here though is that we have no idea what caused a man like Ted Bundy. We have no idea how to track down and capture such a man. Our legal systems are inadequate to prosecute such an individual. Any sentence – even the death penalty – is woefully inadequate to punish such a monster.

Only he was not a monster, but a human being. He moved though society invisibly, indistinguishable from you and me. His victims were women and girls. Other serial killers such as John Wayne Gacy preyed on young boys. Ronald Dominique concentrated on mature men whose bodies he dumped on the roadsides and bayous of Louisiana after sexually abusing and killing them. Then there are those who shoot up schools, cinemas and shopping centres. To those who knew them they all seemed perfectly normal, albeit sometimes a bit eccentric.

If any lesson is to be learned from Ted Bundy, it is that a killer may be sitting next to you at your desk at work right now. Or they may be the lover who is sharing your bed. Or they could even be on the campaign team of your favoured candidate at the next election. Why not the candidate himself or herself? None of us are safe.

CHAPTER ONE
Ted

WOMEN HAD GONE MISSING BEFORE. There had even been murderous attacks. But the police only realized that a serial killer was at large on Sunday 14 July 1974, when two young women disappeared from the picnic area at Lake Sammamish State Park in Washington State on the same day. Others had been approached. There were numerous witnesses and the police even knew the man's name. It was Ted. Before, the attacks had taken place at night. Now the perpetrator had the nerve to carry out his abductions in broad daylight.

A FUN SUNDAY BY THE LAKE TURNS DARK

That Sunday was hot and sunny and the crowd in the park, some 12 miles (19 km) east of Seattle, had swelled to 40,000. A local brewery was holding its annual beer party, complete with music and a keg-throwing contest. Water-skiers were out on the lake. Even the Seattle police were having a picnic there.

Twenty-three-year-old Janice Ott left a note saying 'I am at Lake Sammamish sunin' myself' on the door of her apartment in Issaquah, five miles (8 km) away. Wearing a white blouse knotted at the midriff and a pair of Levi's cut-offs over her black bikini, she rode her yellow ten-speed bike to the park.

Jerry Snyder, a Drug Enforcement Administration (DEA) agent from Seattle, noticed the attractive young blonde spread out a blanket and stripped down to her bikini. He then noticed a young man who had been looking at other young women in the park sit down beside her. The young man had his arm in a sling.

Moments earlier, the same man had approached 22-year-old Janice Graham at the nearby bandstand. She said he was 5 ft 8 in to 5 ft 10 in (173–79 cm), with curly, sandy blond hair, weighed 150–160 lb (68–72 kg) and was 24 or 25 years old. He was wearing white shorts and a white T-shirt with red trim around the neck.

Explaining that he had hurt his arm playing racquetball, he asked her if she could help him unload a sailboat from his car. She agreed and walked with him to the parking lot. They walked up to his metallic brown Volkswagen Beetle, but there was no sign of a boat or a trailer. The sailboat, he said, was at his parents' house just up the hill. She explained that she could not go with him to fetch it as she was waiting for her husband and her folks.

'That's okay,' said the man with the sling. 'I should have told you that it was not in the parking lot. Thanks for bothering.'

Ted Bundy's 1968 VW Beetle in the National Museum of Crime and Punishment. With its cracked windscreen and faded Utah inspection sticker, it takes pride of place in the building's lobby.

Ten minutes later she saw him walking towards the parking lot once more, this time with a blond girl with a yellow ten-speed bike.

Fifteen-year-old Sylvia Valint and two school friends were sunbathing just a few feet from Janice Ott when the man with the sling had approached her. He introduced himself as 'Ted' and asked her whether she could help him with his sailboat. She invited him to sit down. This time he explained that the boat was at his parents' house in Issaquah. Sylvia described him as 'smooth talking'.

Housewife Traci Sharpe was also nearby and was suspicious. 'I didn't feel his arm was really hurt,' she said. 'I do remember he took his arm from the sling and moved it around.'

She did not think that Janice was buying Ted's line. Nevertheless, Traci saw Janice get up and put on her blouse and shorts. The man agreed to introduce her to his parents and teach her to sail. After he assured her that her bike would fit in his VW Beetle, they left together.

Around the time Janice Ott left the park with Bundy, 19-year-old Denise Naslund was leaving Charlie's Eastern Tavern in Seattle with her boyfriend Kenny Little and their friends Nancy Battena and Bob Sargent. They picked up some beers and headed for the park. It was about 12.30 pm. On the way they took some Valium.

Jacqueline Plischke arrived in the park around 4 pm. She was wearing cut-off blue jeans and pink bikini top. As she was locking up her bike she noticed a man was watching her. A little later he approached her and asked if she could help him put his sailboat on his car.

Minutes earlier he had asked 16-year-old Sindi Siebenbaum if she could help him launch his sailboat. She declined, explaining that people were waiting for her. Jacqueline also refused, saying she was waiting for someone. Then he approached Patricia Ann Turner, who explained that she wasn't feeling well – too much sun. The young women he approached said that he spoke with a light accent, perhaps Canadian or British.

Denise Naslund's party had picnicked on hamburgers and hotdogs. Her boyfriend Kenny had fallen asleep. Around 4.40 pm, she got up to go to the restroom. She did not return. Kenny woke about half an hour later and was immediately alarmed. Denise had left her purse in the trunk of her car and she was not the sort of person who went anywhere without her makeup.

Kenny, Nancy and Bob began searching the park. There was no sign of Denise. They continued searching until the crowds thinned out at around 8.30 pm. Kenny then called the police and was told that a person must be missing for 24 hours before an investigation could start. Besides, a relative must file the report, so Kenny drove to Denise's mother's house, and she immediately called the police.

'I know Denise would never take off and leave her car,' she told them. 'She was so happy when I bought it for her. Or leave her purse. She took too much pride in how she looked. I knew something had happened.'

It is thought that Bundy took Denise to where Janice was being kept, tied up but still alive. After repeated sex attacks, first on Ott, then on Naslund, Bundy killed one in front of the other. Two months later, in September 1974, the remains of Janice Ott and Denise Naslund were found with a third unidentified body, dumped in woodland two miles (3 km) east of Lake Sammamish Park. Their killer had returned to have sex with their corpses despite their growing state of putrefaction. Little was left of them when they were found. Their flesh had been eaten by animals. Two of the skulls were missing. Bundy was known to decapitate his victims' corpses and keep their severed heads for oral sex later.

After the bodies were found, the Issaquah Police Department turned the investigation over to Seattle's King County Police Department, which was also looking at a series of possibly related attacks, abduction and murders from the previous year. Seattle is the county seat of King County, Washington.

On 25 November 1973, 15-year-old Kathy Devine had been hitchhiking from Seattle to Oregon. She was seen getting into a pick-up truck with a male driver. On 6 December her body was found by a couple hired to clean up McKenny Park near Washington State's capital Olympia, later a haunt of Bundy. Kathy's body was fully clothed, but found face down with her jeans slit down the back seam from waist to crotch. Bundy liked to rape his victims from behind, either vaginally or anally, while strangling them. The abnormally warm winter meant that Kathy's body was decomposed and it had been ravaged by animals. However, the pathologist's tentative conclusion was that she had been throttled or had her throat cut shortly after she had last been seen. It was also thought she had been sodomized. Before his execution Bundy admitted to picking up a hitchhiker in 1973, raping and murdering her, and leaving her body near Olympia, but he couldn't remember exactly where.

THE 'HELPLESS' PREDATOR TARGETS COLLEGE STUDENTS

Next there was the attack on 18-year-old Joni Lenz, who lived in a basement room of a big old house on 8th Avenue near the University of Washington in Seattle. It was accessible from the outside by a side door that was usually kept locked. On the night of 4 January 1974 Joni went to bed as normal. When she did not appear for breakfast the following morning her housemates thought she was having a lie-in. By mid-afternoon she was not responding to their calls so they went down to check on her. They found her unconscious, her face covered with blood. She had been beaten around the head with a metal bar wrenched from the bed frame. When they pulled back the covers, they found that a speculum had been forced into her vagina, causing terrible internal damage.

She survived, after more than a week in a coma. But when she came round she could not remember anything after ten days before the attack. The blow to the head left her brain damaged for the rest of her life. The police believed that a peeping tom had seen her undressing though the basement window, found the door unlocked, made his way to her bedroom and attacked her.

Twenty-one-year-old psychology student Lynda Ann Healy lived just a few blocks away on 12th Avenue. She had an early morning job as the ski report announcer on a local radio station. On 31 January she made dinner for her housemates, before accompanying them to a nearby club named Dante's. After a couple of pitchers of beer they returned home at around 9.30 pm.

Lynda made an hour-long phone call to her boyfriend, then chatted with a housemate before turning in. She too had a bedroom in the basement, separated by a plywood partition from housemate Karen Skaviem's room. As Karen descended the basement stairs at about 12.45 am that night, she did not check to see if the outside door was locked. Indeed, the front door on the ground floor was also unlocked as the keys had been lost. Before everyone had gone to bed, Bundy admitted later, he had tried the door. Finding it open, he decided to return later after everyone had gone to sleep.

Karen dozed off at around 1.30 am. At 5.30 am she heard Lynda's alarm sounding. At 6.30 am the radio station phoned to ask why Lynda had not come in to work. Karen went into Lynda's room and found the bed made. This was odd. Lynda usually left it unmade because of her early start. But she had not shown up at work that morning and the bike she used to ride there was still in the basement. Nor did she appear in class later.

Housemate Joanne Testa called Lynda's mother at 4 pm. Her father and brother arrived at 6 pm, as Lynda was supposed to cook dinner for the family that evening. The police were called and patrolmen visited to make enquiries. At 8 pm the phone rang, but there was no one on the line. There were two more calls where the caller remained silent.

When homicide detectives arrived and pulled back the covers on Lynda's bed, they found bloodstains. Blood had soaked through the sheets into the mattress. Whoever had shed the blood had been seriously injured, but there was not enough blood present to show that the victim had bled to death.

A pillowcase was missing. In the closet detectives found Lynda's nightdress, which was stiff with dried blood around the collar. The clothes that she had been wearing the previous evening were missing, along with her backpack. The area was searched, but nothing was found. Forensic examination of the crime scene also came up with nothing. The perpetrator had not left so much as a hair, or a drop of blood or semen.

On 4 February someone called 911. A male voice said: 'Listen carefully. The person who attacked that girl on the 8th last month and the person who took Lynda Healy away were one and the same. He was outside both houses. He was seen.' When asked who was calling, the man said: 'No way are you going to get my name,' and hung up.

Lynda's current and former boyfriends volunteered to take lie detector tests and passed. With nothing to go on, the police were stymied. All that was clear was that Lynda was dead. A year later her lower jaw was found on Taylor Mountain, near the Washington Cascades, another of Bundy's dumping grounds. It was identified by dental records.

Nineteen-year-old Donna Manson was a student at Evergreen State College near Olympia in Washington. On the night of 12 March 1974 she planned to attend a jazz concert on campus. She left the dormitory at around 7 pm. Her route would have taken her down a dark pathway. She did not arrive at the concert. No one worried – at first. Donna was a flighty young woman who frequently went missing. The college's chief security officer and the local police were only informed of her absence six days later. Few, if any, of her clothes were missing and she had even left money behind.

Eighteen-year-old Susan Rancourt went missing from Central Washington State College (now Central Washington University) in Ellensburg on 17 April 1974. Like the other victims, she was pretty, with her long blond hair parted in the middle. At 8 pm she had put clothes into one of her dorm's washing machines, before attending a meeting in Munson Hall at the southern end of the campus. Her clothes were still in the machine when Susan's roommate Diana Pitt filed a missing person's report with the campus police department at 5 pm the following day. Nothing was missing from her room. Her route back to the dorm would have taken her down some darkened pathways and she could not see well. Her glasses and contact lenses had been left behind in her room.

'I DIDN'T KNOW HIM. I DIDN'T WANT TO GET INTO HIS CAR.'

However, the suspected abductor had been seen. At around 10 pm, 21-year-old Kathleen D'Olivo was leaving the Bouillon Library, heading for the parking lot, when she heard the sound of books hitting the ground. She turned around to see that they had been dropped by a man with one arm in a metal brace and the other in a sling. Kathleen picked the books up for him. She thought he was going to the library. Instead he was heading for his car, which was parked in a dark no-parking area under a railway bridge surrounded by tall grass. He said he had been injured in a skiing accident, so she carried his backpack for him.

His car was a brown VW Beetle. She put down his backpack and said goodbye. He then fumbled with his car keys, dropped them and asked her to pick them up for him. She was wary. Instead of bending down to grope for them in the darkness, she suggested they step back. What little light there was glinted off the keys. She grabbed them, dropped them in his hand and made off.

At 10.15 pm, another student named Barbara Blair said she saw a young white female wearing a yellow coat with a man in a parka on Walnut Mall, near the library, which would have been on Susan Rancourt's route back to her dorm. They were heading in the direction that Kathleen D'Olivo had taken earlier with the man with his arm in a sling.

Twenty-one-year-old Jane Curtis had a similar encounter three days earlier. She had been leaving the library at around 9 pm. Again the mystery man had dropped his books. When she went to his assistance, he explained that he had been injured in a skiing accident. She carried his books to his car, then he handed her the keys to open the door. Wary, she refused to take them. After he opened the door, he asked her to get in and start the car for him.

'He told me that he was having trouble getting it started and asked me to get in and try the ignition while he did something under the hood,' she said. 'I didn't know him. I didn't want to get in his car, and I just made some excuse about being in a hurry and I left.

Jane dropped his books and fled. But Susan Rancourt did not flee. Her skull was found on Taylor Mountain. It had suffered blunt force trauma to the back of the head and her jawbone was broken in three places.

Nineteen days after Susan Rancourt went missing, on 6 May 21-year-old Roberta Kathleen 'Kathy' Parks disappeared from the Oregon State University campus at Corvallis, over 200 miles (322 km) away. She was studying world religions. Tall and slender, she had her waist-length ash blond hair parted in the middle. She was unhappy because she had recently broken up with her boyfriend and her father had just had a heart attack.

At around 11 pm, after an exercise session in the dorm lounge of her hall of residence, Sackett Hall, she set out for the student union building to get refreshments. She did not arrive. Because of her despondent state, the nearby Willamette River was dragged, in case she had committed suicide. As in previous cases, she had left behind her clothes, cosmetics and her bike.

After a fruitless week-long search her picture went up alongside those of the other missing women and girls on the wall of every law enforcement agency in the Pacific Northwest. Captain Herb Swindler, Commander of Seattle Police Department's Crimes Against Persons Unit, became convinced that Kathy Parks had suffered the same fate as the girls who had gone missing from campuses in Washington State.

Fifteen-year-old Brenda Baker went missing on 25 May 1974 after running away from home in the Seattle suburb of Redmond. Her light brown hair was parted in the middle. Her body was found in Millersylvania State Park, 35 miles (56 km) away, on 17 June. It was so badly decomposed that it was impossible to determine the cause of death.

On 31 May, 22-year-old Brenda Ball spent the evening in the Flame Tavern in Burien near the airport in southern Seattle. A college dropout, she was pretty, with her long dark hair parted in the middle. She left the bar in the early hours of 1 June, intending to hitchhike home. She was never seen again, although Bundy later admitted he was involved in her disappearance. Her skull was found on Taylor Mountain. The right side had sustained a traumatic blunt force injury.

Eighteen-year-old Georgann Hawkins, a student at the University of Washington, had been to a party on 11 June, but left early as she had a Spanish test the following day. She was small, with long brown hair parted in the middle. On the way back to her sorority house she dropped by to see her boyfriend at his fraternity house six doors away. At around 1 am she left to walk the 30 yards (27 m) home. Her roommate Dee Nichols was waiting up for her as she had lost her key to the back door. Several students saw Georgann as she made her way along 17th Avenue NE, known as 'Greek Row' because of the fraternity and sorority houses there. She never arrived at her sorority house, disappearing within a few yards of home.

Anxious, Dee later called Georgann's boyfriend's frat house, only to discover that she had left two hours earlier. Dee woke their housemother, who called the police in the morning. A leading criminologist and three detectives made a fingertip search of the 30 yards (27 m) of 17th Avenue NE she would have traversed, but found nothing.

However, two witnesses came forward. One was a sorority sister who had been walking down 17th Avenue NE at around 12.30 am, when she saw ahead of her a young man on crutches. One leg of his jeans had been cut open to reveal a plaster cast.

He was carrying a briefcase which he kept dropping. She offered to carry it for him, but said she had to go into the sorority house for a moment first, if he did not mind waiting. She was a little longer than she thought and when she came out he had gone.

A male student also saw a young man on crutches. He was with a girl with her hair parted in the middle and carrying a briefcase. He was shown a photograph of Georgann Hawkins, but was sure that it was not her.

'THEY CALL ME GEORGE'

Detective Bob Keppel with the King County Sheriff's Department worked on the Bundy case and interviewed him later on Death Row, where he revealed little known facts about the abduction and murder of Georgann Hawkins. Bundy had, apparently, rehearsed the abduction two weeks earlier when he had lured a pretty woman from the sorority house down an alley behind Greek Row to an unlit parking lot. There he had thanked her before driving to his home, which was just five blocks away.

As Georgann was saying goodbye to a friend at the window of her boyfriend's frat house, Bundy had hobbled through the darkness on his crutches, carrying a briefcase full of books and feigning some difficulty. He saw her walking along the north end of the block and was just 60 ft (18 m) from the back door of the sorority house when he approached her out of the shadows. She smiled. He dropped the briefcase and asked her if she would carry it for him. She obliged.

'They call me George,' she said.

They walked up the dark alley to the unlit parking lot. Bundy had already placed a crowbar and handcuffs on the ground near the rear of his car. When they reached his VW Beetle, she unsuspectingly turned her back on him. He grabbed the crowbar and struck her on the back of the head so hard that her earrings and one of her shoes flew off. Her knees buckled and she sank to the ground, unconscious. Quickly he handcuffed her wrists and loaded her into the passenger side of the car, where the passenger seat had been removed. Then he got into the driver's seat and drove away.

He headed out of Seattle past Issaquah. Suddenly he heard babbling. Georgann had regained consciousness.

'At this point she was quite lucid, talking about things, about some – it's funny, it's not funny but it's odd the kinds of things people will say and under those circumstances,' Bundy said. 'And she thought … she said that she thought that she had a Spanish test the next day and she thought that I had taken her to help tutor me for her Spanish test.'

He drove on to his Issaquah killing site, where Janice Ott and Denise Naslund already lay dead. Stopping at a grassy patch at the end of a dirty road, he pulled Georgann's struggling body out of the car, lay her on the ground and knocked her out again with the crowbar. Her 'babbling' stopped.

Inside the car was a black bag that carried his murder kit. He pulled out a piece of rope, wrapped it around her neck and tightened it until her breathing stopped. Then he pulled her into a small grove of trees. He spent the rest of the night there, holding her naked body.

In the morning, he said, the shock and horror of what he had done struck him. He left the body where it was and bundled everything else into his car and drove off. Along the way he threw her clothes out of the window, along with the crutches, the briefcase and the rope.

That afternoon he returned to check that he had got rid of everything. Retracing his route, he found everything except one of her shoes. This, he figured, must have been left in the parking lot where he had clubbed her and stuffed her into the car. Realizing that the police would be looking for someone with a car, he returned to the crime scene on a bicycle and recovered her shoe, along with her earrings.

Three days later Bundy returned to commit necrophilia with Georgann's corpse. Then, he said, he cut off her head with a hacksaw and buried it 50 ft (15m) further up the road. It was never found.

CHAPTER TWO
Theodore

TED BUNDY was born Theodore Robert Cowell on 24 November 1946 in Burlington, Vermont. His father was said to be a sailor named Jack Worthington who had recently returned from fighting in the Second World War. He had nothing further to do with his son.

The boy's mother, Louise Cowell, gave birth in the Elizabeth Lund Home for Unwed Mothers. There were no complications and he was a healthy baby. After he was born she returned to her family in Philadelphia. To avoid the shame surrounding illegitimacy at the time his grandparents masqueraded as his parents and pretended that his mother Louise was his sister.

EVIDENCE OF ABUSE?

Bundy later insisted that he worshipped his grandfather. However, when psychiatrist Dr Dorothy Otnow Lewis, a

To avoid the stigma of illegitimacy, Bundy's grandparents pretended to be his parents. The problem was, his grandfather was 'an extremely violent and frightening individual'.

specialist in violent behaviour, examined him on Death Row, she said that he had been 'horribly traumatized'. His grandfather Samuel Cowell was 'an extremely violent and frightening individual,' she said. He also kept a collection of pornography in the greenhouse, which young Ted had access to. His grandmother also suffered from psychotic depression and agoraphobia, and was given electroshock therapy.

According to Bundy's aunt Julia, who was 12 when he was born, her nephew was deeply disturbed from an early age. From the age of three 'he would take up butcher knives from the kitchen and come upstairs and secretly lift up her covers and place them in beside her on her double bed,' Dr Lewis recalls her saying.

This 'extraordinarily bizarre behaviour,' added Dr Lewis, was 'the kind of behaviour that to the best of my knowledge you only see in youngsters who themselves have been seriously traumatized, who have either themselves been the victims of extraordinary abuse, or who have witnessed extreme violence among family members.'

In 1951 Ted and his mother went to live with his uncle Jack Cowell in Tacoma, Washington State. First, Ted's last name was changed to Nelson. It is thought that his mother did not want him ridiculed for sharing a surname with his great uncle and his mother, again indicating that he was illegitimate.

Later that year Louise met John Bundy, a mild-mannered North Carolinian who had settled in Washington and worked as a cook at Madigan Hospital in Fort Lewis. They married, he adopted Ted and the child's name was changed again. They lived for some time in the countryside, but returned to Tacoma in time for Ted to begin school. The Bundys then had four more children – two girls and two boys. Ted got on well with his siblings and said he loved his stepfather, but when they argued Ted would get the better of the argument as he was more intellectually adept.

It was around this time Ted discovered that he was illegitimate, either by coming across his birth certificate or being shown it maliciously by a cousin. This disturbed him immensely throughout his life. According to a pre-sentence report in 1976: 'It is of interest that the defendant displayed marked signs of hostility when asked about his early childhood. Specifically when asked about his real father's whereabouts, his face became quite contorted and he replied succinctly and approximately: "You might say that he left my mother and me and never rejoined the family."'

The report also said that in the fourth grade he had a teacher who was a 'voluptuous disciplinarian'. It was also said that at Hunt Junior High Ted would masturbate in the broom cupboard. When schoolmates discovered this they pulled the door open and threw cold water on him. His early sexual behaviour made him the butt of relentless teasing. His poor academic performance and failure to get himself elected student vice president brought further humiliation. By the time he went to Wilson High School he was the archetypal loner, consoling himself with sport – particularly skiing.

He had a paper round and earned money cutting people's lawns, using access to their homes as an opportunity for petty theft and possibly worse. On the night of 31 August 1961, 8-year-old Ann Marie Burr went missing from her home in Tacoma while her parents and little sister slept. The police and 150 soldiers searched for her the next day. She was never found. An intruder had entered through a living room window, leaving behind grass clippings. On Death Row in 1987, Bundy made reference to the killing. He had lived just three miles (5 km) away and an uncle lived close to where the little girl took piano lessons.

A COLLEGE BOY WITHOUT A SOCIAL LIFE

When Bundy graduated from high school in 1965, he enrolled at the University of Puget Sound in Tacoma, Washington, continuing to live at home while dreaming of having a relationship with a beautiful co-ed, but not knowing how to get one. His social life consisted of attending class and hanging out with two male friends from school.

The following year he enrolled at the University of Washington to study Asian history and Chinese. There he met his dream co-ed, known after Bundy's rise to notoriety by the pseudonym Stephanie Brooks. She was older than Bundy and came from a wealthy family, but they shared a passion for skiing. Bundy made an effort to measure up to her expectations, but the relationship became strained when he began to fail academically, and she dumped him.

Bundy took time out in San Francisco, Denver, Philadelphia and Arkansas before returning to Washington State, where he occasionally saw Stephanie, although they were no longer together. He took a number of menial jobs. Then he threw himself into the Republican campaign to elect Pasco City Councilman Arthur Fletcher as the first black Lieutenant Governor of Washington State. Fletcher's campaign failed, but Bundy was named 'Mr up-and-coming Republican'. Meanwhile, Bundy was pursuing his other interests as a peeping tom.

In January 1969 he enrolled in Temple University in Philadelphia. It is thought that it was there that he began his career in stalking, which would culminate in rape and murder. He bought a wig and a false moustache to disguise himself. He also trawled the streets of New York and, according to his own account, in Ocean City, New Jersey, he tried to abduct a woman but she escaped. In future, he vowed, he would be better prepared. On Death Row, Bundy claimed to have killed two women while living in Philadelphia.

After a few months Bundy returned to Washington State, renting a small apartment on 12th Avenue NE in Seattle's university district. His landlords, Ernst and Frieda Rogers, found him polite and helpful. Another tenant said that he sounded British, 'having a clipped, concise diction similar to an Englishman who had been Americanized'. To pay the rent Bundy took a job in a lumber mill, then became a legal messenger.

On 30 September 1969 he was at the Sandpiper Tavern in the university district and asked a young woman named Elizabeth Kendall to dance. She refused and he went to dance with someone else. Later, though, she went over to talk to him. She was from Utah, newly divorced, with a young daughter. He said he was writing a book about the Vietnam war. He was not, but she was taken with his accent, which she took to be British.

They left the Sandpiper Tavern together and went to pick up her daughter Tina from the babysitter's. Bundy stayed the night. A little drunk, they slept with their clothes on, but it was the beginning of a relationship that would last six years.

Liz visited his family in Tacoma and he spent Christmas with her at her parents' house in Utah. They liked him and there was talk of marriage. He was a permanent fixture in her apartment. If they were together, she said she could help pay for his law school. She was under the impression that he wanted to be a lawyer, but the following June, he re-enrolled at the University of Washington, this time majoring in psychology.

He graduated with a BSc two years later. While there, he offered his services to the campus police as an informant on radical anti-war groups that proliferated at the time.

Meanwhile, he continued working for the Republican Party and became a counsellor at the Seattle Crisis Clinic, where he met Ann Rule, a former cop who became a crime writer and was commissioned to write about the Bundy murders before Bundy was unmasked. She said that on more than one occasion he helped prevent a suicide. He also continued his career as a peeping tom, masturbating outside basement windows while women undressed inside.

To support himself while at university Bundy took a job as a delivery driver for a medical supplies company. During the five months he worked there he stole crutches, plaster of Paris, which he used to make casts, and the speculum he later forced into Joni Lenz's vagina. He then took a job counselling at the Harborview Mental Health Center in Seattle and, while Liz was away visiting her parents in Utah, had an affair with a co-worker. They would take long drives out into remote areas beyond Lake Sammamish. However, the job foundered when it was reported that Bundy was 'not capable of being emotionally responsive to the needs of his clients and patients'.

When Liz returned from Utah, Bundy's affair with the other woman continued. Liz became upset and he summarily broke off the liaison to make up with Liz. She forgave him, although his habitual stealing continued to trouble her. A friend spotted him roaming around the rear of a house, looking through windows, and assumed he was looking for things to steal. Liz then caught him trying to conceal a pair of surgical gloves.

In 1973 Bundy was accepted to law school at the University of Utah at his second attempt, thanks to a letter from Governor Dan Evans, whose campaign he had worked on. He met up with Stephanie Brooks again and she was impressed. He asked her to marry him. She accepted. However, he had no intention of doing so, and simply abandoned her to get his own back for her dumping him earlier.

He worked briefly for the Seattle Crime Commission, where the director said he was 'well dressed, intelligent and acted extremely proper at all times'. He wrote a report on sexual assaults on women, detailing how the attacks were made and how the various law enforcement agencies worked together, or failed to. Moving on to the King County Law and Justice Planning Office, he took the opportunity to do more research into how police and sheriffs offices handled investigations. This was invaluable once he began killing in earnest.

In May 1973 he went to work for the Republican State Central Committee in Olympia, Washington State, where he became good friends with his boss. That summer Bundy decided not to move to Utah to take up his place in the law school there, and instead enrolled at the newly opened School of Law at the University of Puget Sound in Tacoma. He did not do well and, in December, decided that his future lay in Utah after all.

Working at the Department of Emergency Services in Olympia, Bundy would play racquetball at Evergreen State College, where in March he would kill Donna Manson. By then his attendance at law school was dropping off. Eventually he would drop out.

'He couldn't concentrate... he didn't understand why,' said Liz. 'Being a lawyer meant everything to him, but he was terribly afraid that he wasn't going to make it.'

His commitment to the Republican Party also waned. As well as paying for Bundy's legal studies, Liz bought him a raft and he went rafting with a woman named Becky Gibbs and some friends down the Yakima River, which passes by Ellensburg, where Susan Rancourt would go missing, and through some of Washington State's wildest country, which he seemed to know quite well. As well as performing some dangerous antics to scare her, he suddenly undid the straps of Becky's halter top, leaving her very embarrassed.

He also went rafting with Liz and one time he suddenly pushed her overboard into the icy water.

'I looked up at Ted and our eyes locked,' she said. 'His face had gone blank, as though he was not there at all. I had the sense that he wasn't seeing me. I struggled to pull myself into the raft. He didn't move, he didn't speak. I could find no expression on his face.'

There were other incidents. When Liz noticed that he had a new television, stereo and typewriter, she accused him, once again, of being a thief. He grabbed her by her arm. 'If you ever tell anyone about this,' he said, 'I'll break your f***ing neck.'

Later that night he turned up at her place crying, saying he didn't understand why he had taken those things. He swore he would not steal anymore.

Unexpectedly, he demanded anal sex with her. She refused, but allowed him to tie her up. When she put an end to this too, he went off sex with her altogether. Liz was also surprised when she learned that Ted had been to Lake Sammamish on 7 July. They had never been there together and neither, as far as she knew, had he been there before, and she did not know what prompted his interest.

The following Saturday she called him at his parents' house in Tacoma and asked if he wanted to do something the next day – Sunday 14 July, the day Janice Ott and Denise Naslund went missing. He said he had other things to do.

'What other things?' asked Liz.

'Just other things, Liz,' he said.

However, he did turn up at her apartment the following morning while she was getting ready to go to church. She was planning to spend the afternoon in Carkeek Park and expected Ted to meet her there. He did not show up. Clearly he had other things to do. But he did phone that evening and took her to dinner. He was ravenous and clearly exhausted by the events of the day. On Monday and Tuesday, he skipped work.

FIRST SUSPICIONS?

While the disappearance of Bundy's earlier victims had quickly faded in the press, the abduction of two women from Lake Sammamish Park on a single day persisted. And the media now had a name – 'Ted' – which he gave not just to Janice Ott, but to other women who had refused to go with him. They also had solid descriptions of him and his car. It was the perfect time for him to move on to Salt Lake City, Utah.

Liz's parents found him a room near the university, although Liz herself decided to stay in Seattle. Although she was worried that he might be unfaithful to her there, she was confident that their relationship would endure and he would return to her when he graduated.

Meanwhile the newspapers were beginning to tie the disappearance of Janice Ott and Denise Naslund to the other girls who had gone missing earlier, and Liz began to notice disturbing similarities between her Ted and the Lake Sammamish Park suspect. Both had VW Beetles and spoke with an accent thought to be British. He kept crutches in his room and she remembered finding plaster of Paris in a drawer in his apartment – he said you never knew when you were going to break your leg. And when he moved to Salt Lake City the abductions in Washington State stopped.

Liz made a number of anonymous calls to Seattle Police Department. In October, after the first of the bodies had been found, Liz called the King County police and told them of her suspicions. Asked why she was calling, she said that a friend who had just returned from Utah had told her that girls had begun to go missing there.

Ann Rule had already contacted the police, and a woman who had worked with Bundy at the Department of Emergency Services in Olympia, Washington, recognized him from the artist's impression that the police circulated. Then one of Bundy's psychology professors reported his suspicions but, as Bundy was then a law student, the police thought him an unlikely suspect. However, the call from Liz Kendall did put him into their top 100.

CHAPTER THREE
Utah

BEFORE TED BUNDY left Washington State for Salt Lake City in Utah on 2 September 1974, it is thought that he killed two more women. Twenty-year-old Carol Valenzuela was last seen hitchhiking near Vancouver in Washington State on 2 August. Her remains were discovered two months later in a shallow grave south of Olympia, along with those of another female later identified as 17-year-old Martha Morrison, last seen in Eugene, Oregon, on 1 September 1974. Both victims had long hair parted in the middle. Bundy's route to Salt Lake City could have taken him through Vancouver and Eugene. However, serial killer, rapist and torturer Warren Leslie Forrest was also active in the area at the time.

On his way to Utah Bundy called Liz Kendall from Nampa, Idaho, to tell her he loved her. Twenty miles further on, as he was entering the city of Boise, he spotted a young woman hitchhiking. She was, he thought, 16 or 18 years old. He stopped and she got in. The interstate was under construction at the time, so Bundy had an excuse to pull off the main highway and use an older road that ran along the river. Choosing his moment, he pulled a crowbar from under the passenger seat and clubbed her around the head, caving in her skull.

She was still alive when her dragged her out of the car and pulled her clothes off. He strangled her while sodomizing her. The sight of a fresh corpse always aroused him and he had sex with her dead body probably twice more. Then he dropped her and her clothes into the river after destroying her ID. He telephoned Liz again when he arrived in Salt Lake City early the next morning.

Bundy's attendance at law school was poor, as he spent his time planning fresh abductions and murders. In just six weeks he would kidnap and kill four young women.

On the evening of 2 October, 16-year-old cheerleader Nancy Wilcox disappeared from Holladay, Utah, on the outskirts of Salt Lake City.

Her blond hair was parted in the middle and she was last seen in a VW Beetle, described by a witness as 'yellow'. On Death Row, Bundy admitted killing her, although he said he didn't mean to. He saw her walking down a darkened street and claimed that he only intended to sexually assault her.

Parking his car, he grabbed a knife and ran up behind her. He forced her into a dark orchard and tried to pull off her clothes. When she objected, he choked her, again claiming that he only wanted her to pass out rather than expire. Once she was quiet, he stripped her, took off his own clothes and had sex with her. He left her there, but returned a couple of hours later to check she was dead. Her body was never found.

ONE POTENTIAL VICTIM ESCAPES BUNDY'S CLUTCHES

Nine days later, 21-year-old student Rhonda Stapley was travelling back to the campus of the University of Utah after a dental appointment when a tan Volkswagen pulled up at the bus stop.

'The cute driver leaned over, rolled down the passenger window and asked where I was going,' she said.

'Up to the U.'

'Me too,' he said. 'Hop in.'

She opened the door and got in.

'The possibility that this man could be dangerous did not enter my mind,' she said. 'He was handsome and clean cut, and I felt certain he was a college student – a friendly student helping out a fellow student.'

Nevertheless, Rhonda was all too well aware of the dangers.

'I would never have dreamed of hitchhiking – of sticking out my thumb so that a random stranger could pick me up. That was dangerous. Everyone knew that,' she said. 'But this was different. Accepting a ride from this well-groomed young man did not seem risky or wrong.'

In the car, she told him her name was Rhonda and she was studying pharmacy. He introduced himself as Ted and said he was a first-year law student.

She soon noticed that he did not follow the regular route back to the campus, but he said he had an errand to run up near the zoo. 'Ted looked like a typical university student,' she said. 'He had slightly curly dark brown hair, a nice complexion, and his smile was friendly and inviting. He wore dark slacks and a green pullover sweater, not unlike what I would expect to see on a law student on his way to or from a class. He was polite. He didn't talk much, but when he did his voice was confident, his conversation articulate and on subject.'

When they got to the zoo he drove straight past it and continued up Emigration Canyon into Parley's Canyon.

'It was obvious he had no errand to run,' she said, 'but I was not worried. I just figured he was taking me on a little ride. It felt sort of flirtatious.'

At the end of Parley's Canyon he should have turned right, back towards the campus. Instead he turned left and drove up another deserted canyon. Rhonda began to get nervous. Bundy had stopped talking. He drove silently, gripping the wheel. He made no contribution to the conversations, and even though Rhonda tried to keep it going he did not nod or respond in any way.

He slowed on the corners of the twisting road, as if hunting for a picnic spot.

'I thought that he must be looking for a place to "park",' she said, 'and I was uncomfortable with the idea.' Her mouth was sore from the dentist. 'I knew that kissing would only make it worse. Besides, I hardly knew this man, and I wasn't really a "make-out" kind of girl.'

On the other hand, she did not want to offend the cute law student and tried to think up excuses for not stopping. As the sun sank low in the sky, he found a place that suited him. He pulled off the road into a wooded area where there was a picnic table.

Stopping the car, he turned off the engine, turned towards her and leaned in close.

'I was nervous he was going to kiss me,' she said. 'I didn't want to kiss him, but I didn't know how to get out of the situation without embarrassing myself by making a fuss.'

With his face inches from hers, he said quietly: 'Do you know what? I am going to kill you.' He put his hands around her throat and started squeezing.

Hours passed before she regained consciousness. She found herself sprawled out on the ground, face down in the dirt, surprised to be alive.

It was now completely dark, with the scene lit only by the interior light of the VW shining out of the open door. Bundy stood there, fiddling with something behind the seat.

Barely conscious and terrified, Rhonda realized that this was her chance to escape. Pumping adrenaline, she jumped up and ran into the darkness. But her trousers were still around her ankles and she tripped and fell. For a moment she felt as if she was suspended in mid-air, then found herself in ice-cold water. She had fallen into a fast-flowing mountain stream. This carried her away from her attacker, but now she feared she was going to drown.

Then she hit a tangle of tree limbs and pulled herself out of the water. Cold and wet, she made her way across the rough terrain, following the course of the river, figuring that Salt Lake

City was downstream. She pressed on, constantly worrying that the monster who had attacked her was following. Eventually she came across a road. It took her all night to walk home.

Rhonda did not think about reporting what had happened to the police. A Mormon, she was frightened that if her mother found out she was no longer a virgin she would take her out of college. She washed herself over and over again and vowed that no one would ever know what had happened to her.

When Bundy was finally arrested Rhonda recognized that he was the man who had abducted and raped her. She felt guilty that other women had been attacked because she had not reported her assault, but it was clear that she was suffering from post-traumatic stress disorder. For 37 years she kept quiet. Then in 2011, after a workplace confrontation with a bullying boss, it all came back to her.

After communication online with another survivor of a brush with Bundy, Rhonda went into therapy. She kept a journal which was published as *I Survived Ted Bundy* in 2016. It had a foreword by Ann Rule, who by then had published her own account as *The Stranger Beside Me*.

The victim that alerted the authorities in Utah to the presence of the serial killer was Melissa Smith, the 17-year-old daughter of the Chief of Police in Midvale in Salt Lake County. She had long brown hair, parted in the middle, and went missing some time after 10 pm on 18 October 1974. In the seven weeks Bundy had been in Utah, he had driven hundreds of miles to familiarize himself with the area, finding dumping grounds and searching for victims.

Melissa Smith disappeared on a Friday night when she was due to attend a sleepover at a friend's house. But the sleepover had been cancelled. No one had told her, her ride did not turn up, and when she called the friend's house the phone just rang out. However, another friend who had just broken up with her boyfriend called and Melissa agreed to meet her at a nearby pizza parlour. She walked there. It was in nearby State Street, where the shops and restaurants attracted young people after dark – just the sort of place Bundy would hunt for prey.

At around 9 pm Melissa phoned home and told her sister Jolene that she would be back at around 10 pm. That was the last time anyone heard from her. A witness saw her hitchhiking, even though her father had warned her not to do so. She may, however, have continued homewards on foot. A short cut would have taken her down a dirt road, along a dirt bank, under a highway overpass and a railway bridge, and across a school playing field where there was no lighting. A local resident raking up leaves in their front yard heard a scream at around 10.15 pm.

Liz Kendall talked to Bundy on the phone that night. He was planning to go hunting with her dad the next day and was in a good mood. She had no reason to think that anything was amiss.

On the afternoon of 27 October Melissa's body, naked except for a necklace of wooden beads, was found by deer hunters in Summit Park, 12 miles (19 km) east of Salt Lake City in the Wasatch Mountains. Her face was so badly battered that even her father failed to recognize her.

Her skull was fractured and there was massive internal bleeding. The damage was so extensive that the first detectives on the scene thought she had been shot. Her body was covered with bruises, which had been inflicted prior to death. Other cuts and abrasions showed that her dead body had been dragged across the rough terrain before being dumped. There was only small amount of blood under the body, also indicating that she had been killed elsewhere.

The post-mortem revealed that she had been raped and sodomized. A man's blue sock around her neck had been used to strangle her. This had been tightened so savagely that it broke the hyoid bone in her neck. Even more disturbing was that although Melissa had been missing for nine days, she had only died 36 hours before she was found.

Not only had she been kept, she had been cared for – even though, due to her head wounds, she would almost certainly have been unconscious throughout. Her hair and body had been washed. Her nails had been painted and eye make-up freshly applied. Creepily, neither the nail varnish nor the eye make-up was Melissa's, according to her sister Jolene.

Another abduction occurred on the night of Halloween. The victim was Laura Aime. She was 17, almost 6 ft (183 cm) tall and had her long brown hair parted in the middle. After the murder of Melissa Smith her parents had warned her against hitchhiking. But she did not live with them at home in Salem, Utah, any more. After dropping out of school she went to live in American Fork, 25 miles (40 km) away, although she kept in regular contact with her folks by phone.

She had been to a Halloween party in Orem, Utah, but around midnight set off alone to hitchhike to Lehi, 10 miles (16 km) north up Route 89. It was cold and she was wearing blue jeans, a sweater and a coat with a hood. That was the last that was seen of her.

Her parents did not know that she had gone missing until four days later. They only began to worry when she did not turn up for a hunting trip she had planned to take with her father. When they called her friends to find out why she had not been in touch, they were told that she hadn't been seen since she left the party on Halloween.

Laura's body was found on 27 November by hikers taking a Thanksgiving Day ramble up American Fork Canyon in the Wasatch Mountains. It lay on a river bank below a parking lot. She was naked and, again, her face was so badly battered that her father did not recognize her at first. He identified her from scars on her forearm from a childhood accident. Her discovery was entirely fortuitous. It was unusually mild that Autumn, and the spot where she lay would normally have been covered with snow.

There were depressed fractures of the skull on the left side and the back of her head, and she had been strangled. Again, she was wearing only a necklace. This was tangled up with the nylon stocking used to throttle her. She had been sexually assaulted in the vagina and anus. The wall of her vagina had also been punctured by what was thought to be a metal instrument. Immotile sperm was found, but it was too old to identify the blood type of the man it came from, and DNA profiling was not available then. Blood tests revealed no sign of drugs, although she would have been mildly intoxicated when she died. Like Melissa, Laura's hair had been freshly shampooed.

BUNDY MASQUERADES AS A POLICE OFFICER

By the time Laura was found, Bundy had attempted another abduction. At 6.30 pm on 8 November 1974, 18-year-old Carol DaRonch left home in her new Chevrolet Camaro to go shopping at the Fashion Place Shopping Mall on State Street, where it passes through the suburb of Murray. Although she had graduated that spring and taken a job with the Mountain Bell Telephone Company, Carol still lived at home with her parents. It was beginning to rain as she drove into the parking lot. A pretty young woman, she had long brown hair parted in the middle.

Carol entered the mall through the Sears store on the south side. The place was full of Christmas shoppers. She headed for Auerbach's department store. On the way she ran into some cousins and they had a chat. Carol then made her purchases at Auerbach's and was browsing in Walden's Book Store when she was approached by a handsome young man who, she said, was between 5 ft 7 in and 6 ft (170–83 cm) tall, with long dark brown hair and a neatly trimmed moustache. He wore a sports jacket, green slacks and patent leather shoes.

He asked if she had parked her car in the parking lot by the Sears store. She nodded. He asked her for the licence number. When she told him he appeared to recognize it. He explained that a shopper had reported seeing a man trying to break into her car with a wire coat hanger.

Carol DaRonch testifies at a pre-sentencing hearing for convicted murderer Ted Bundy in Miami in 1979 as Judge Cowart listens behind her. Bundy was convicted of kidnapping DaRonch from a Salt Lake City suburb in 1974.

'Would you mind coming with me so we can check to see if anything has been stolen?' he asked.

Carol assumed that he was a security guard or a policeman. She was a law-abiding citizen and predisposed to comply with authority. It did not occur to her to wonder how the man had recognized her as the driver of the Camaro. She meekly followed him into the rain as he explained that his partner might already have arrested the thief.

'Perhaps you'll recognize him if you see him,' he said.

Believing the man to be a police officer, she asked to see his ID. He chuckled and she felt embarrassed even to have asked.

When they reached the car there was no sign that anyone had tampered with it. Even so, he asked Carol to open the car and check. She opened the driver's door and took a look.

'It's all here,' she said. 'There's nothing missing. I don't think he managed to get in.'

He then asked her to open the passenger door. She said there was no point, as nothing was missing. He tried the door anyway. As he did so, she spotted a pair of shiny handcuffs in the inside pocket of his jacket.

Saying he would have to confer with his partner, he led her back towards the mall.

'They must have gone back to our sub-station,' he said. 'We'll meet them there and identify him.'

'How would I know him?' she asked. 'I wasn't even there. I was inside, shopping.'

He took no notice and walked briskly through the mall and out into the northern parking lot. Carol was beginning to find this tiresome and asked him his name.

'Officer Roseland, Murray Police Department,' he said.

They reached a door with the number 139 on it. This, he explained, was the police sub-station. In fact, it was the back door of a laundromat. He tried the door. It was locked.

He then insisted that she accompany him to police head-quarters to sign a complaint. He said he would drive her there. His car was parked just 10 yards (9 m) away. But instead of giving her a lift in a squad car, he had a battered old VW Beetle parked in the street. It did not look like the sort of car even a plain-clothes policeman would be driving and she asked, again, to see his ID. He pulled out his wallet and flashed what appeared to be a shiny badge. But he did it so fast that it was impossible to read the name of the police department or the badge number.

Reluctantly, Carol got into his car. When the door was closed she smelled alcohol on his breath. Surely policemen were not allowed to drink on duty? He told her to put her seatbelt on. She refused, so she could make a quick escape if necessary. Buckling up was not a legal requirement at the time, as wearing a seat belt only became compulsory in Utah in 1986.

Instead of heading straight on to State Street and towards Murray Police Department, he did a u-turn and headed in the opposite direction. She wondered whether to scream or try to jump out of the car, but they were going too fast. Looking over at him, she noticed that the charm was gone. The smile had disappeared too. His jaw was set and his eyes seemed distant.

Suddenly he bounced the car up on to the sidewalk outside McMillan Grade School and came to an abrupt halt. She grabbed the door handle and tried to jump out. But he was too quick for her and clapped a handcuff on her right wrist.

'What are you doing?' she yelled. 'Let me go!'

She kicked out at him and flailed her arms, scratching him and screaming at the top of her lungs. He fought to get the other handcuff on. But in the confusion he put it on the same wrist.

He was growing angry now, and pulled a small black gun from his pocket. Holding it to her head, he said: 'If you don't stop screaming, I'm going to kill you. I'll blow your brains out.'

CHAPTER THREE

This only made her struggle all the harder. She fell backwards out of the car. He dropped the gun and grabbed a crowbar. Leaping from the car, he grabbed her and pushed her up against the side of the VW Beetle. He raised the crowbar as if to strike her, but she grabbed his wrist and prevented it from crashing down on her head. Then she kicked him in the genitals and fled. He thought of chasing after her, but it was too risky. So he jumped back into his car and sped away.

Wilbur and Mary Walsh were driving down Third Avenue East when Carol ran into their headlights. Wilbur slammed on the brakes and barely missed her. For a moment they thought they were being attacked by a maniac and tried to lock the doors. It was too late. Carol pulled open Mary's door and jumped in.

They could see immediately that Carol was not dangerous. She was terrified and Mrs Walsh tried to comfort her.

'I can't believe it,' she said. 'A man… a man… he was going to kill me.'

They drove her to Murray Police Station on State Street. When they got there Carol was unable to walk, so Mr Walsh carried her in. Through her sobs she told the police that one of their men – Officer Roseland – had attacked her. But they had no Officer Roseland in the department. Nor did any of their police officers use an old Volkswagen while on duty. Carol then held up the handcuffs that were still attached to her right wrist. They were not the Smith & Wesson cuffs generally used by police officers, but Gerocal, a brand made in Taiwan.

The police unlocked them and dusted them for fingerprints. This rendered only a few useless smudges. Outside McMillan

Grade School the police found one of Carol's shoes, dislodged in the struggle, but Bundy's VW was long gone. Carol gave a good description of it. She had even noticed a tear in the upholstery of the back seat, but it could not be found. Nor could any fingerprints be found on the rear door of the laundromat. The door handle had been washed clean by the rain.

Carol trawled her way through books of mug shots, but Bundy had no criminal record. She had never seen him before and there was no clue to his identity. A few days later she discovered a spot of blood on the fur collar of her jacket. The police lab found that it was not hers. It was type O, but there was not enough to determine whether it was rhesus positive or negative. Again, DNA testing was not available back then.

However, Murray Police Department now had a good description of the attacker and his car. Carol had survived and it was clear to detectives that her assailant was the same man who had abducted and killed Melissa Smith, who had last been seen at a pizza parlour only a mile from Fashion Place Mall.

ON THE SAME NIGHT AN ABDUCTION AT A SCHOOL MUSICAL

Carol DaRonch may have escaped alive, but Bundy's appetite had not been sated. He needed more prey. Over the previous two weeks he had checked out the town of Bountiful, Utah, just 17 miles (27 km) north of Murray up the Interstate 15 (I-15) highway. He had seen a flyer for the musical *The Redhead*, which was being performed at Viewmont High School the same night of his failed abduction of Carol DaRonch. The parking lot was full as an audience of 1,500 had turned out. Later, a young woman reported being approached there by a strange man. After a few words, he had walked away.

Bundy entered the lobby of the school and hung around the doors that led to the auditorium. He stopped Raelynne Shepard, the 24-year-old drama teacher at Viewmont High. Later, she told the police about the strange but 'very good looking' man who had approached her. He wore a sports jacket, dress slacks and patent leather shoes.

He was courteous, almost apologetic, and asked her to come out to the parking lot to identify a car. This made little sense to her, and she said she was much too busy.

'It will only take a minute,' he said.

'No, I can't. I'm in charge of the play,' she said, as she hurried on past him.

Twenty minutes later she saw him again, loitering in the lobby.

'Did you find anyone to help you?' she asked.

He said nothing, and merely stared at her. She thought this was strange. But then she was a good-looking woman fresh out of college and was used to men staring.

She then disappeared backstage. When she reappeared a few minutes later, the man was still there. He came up to her, smiling.

'Hey, you look really nice,' he said. Even though he told her he liked her long hair, he kept his eyes on her breasts. 'Come on, give me a hand with that car. Just a couple of minutes will do it.'

Although he was perfectly charming, something about his manner put her on guard. He stood in front of her and tried to block her passage. She pushed past him, saying that maybe her husband could help.

'I'll go and find him,' she said, as she disappeared.

The encounter had frightened her, even though there were several hundred people nearby. His presence there made no sense. The audience was made up of the family and friends of the cast, along with their classmates. He wasn't on the staff. He was too old to be a student and too young to be a parent. Later, she saw him in the auditorium, watching the play alone.

Also in the audience was 17-year-old Debra Kent, whose friend Jolynne Beck had spotted the handsome man too. Debra was there with her father Dean, an oil executive who had recently had a heart attack, and her mother Belva. Debra's 11-year-old brother Blair did not care to see the play, so they had dropped him off at a roller skating rink on the way. They said they would pick him up around 10 pm, when the show was over.

At the intermission it was clear that the play was running late. Belva Kent called the Rustic Roller Rink, but they would not page Blair. Instead, Debra volunteered to go and get her brother. While she was telling her parents this, Bundy was seen pacing back and forth nearby.

After Debra left the building, no one saw her again. Two short piercing screams were heard from the parking lot and Bundy reappeared in the auditorium, looking dishevelled. It is thought that he knocked Debra out in his usual fashion and stashed her body in his VW Beetle, before returning, possibly to throw off the scent anyone who had seen him leave soon after Debra. When Raelynne Shepard pointed out the strange man she had encountered before to a colleague, Bundy noticed their interest and got up and left the auditorium for the last time.

Debra's brother Blair was left stranded at the skating rink. When her parents came out, they found Debra's car had not moved from where they had left it in the parking lot. They searched until midnight, before calling the Bountiful Police Department. In the description they gave of their daughter, they mentioned that she had long brown hair parted in the middle.

'She just wouldn't have left us stranded,' her mother said. 'Her father's just getting over a heart attack and the car's still at the school. It doesn't make sense.'

Twenty-five years later Belva Kent recalled the moment they saw that Debra's car was still in the parking lot.

'That was when we really panicked,' she said. 'It was a terrible night, and from then on, it never stopped.'

Patrol cars circled the school while every room was opened and searched, in case she had been locked in. In the morning the police searched the parking lot and found a small key, recognizing it immediately as the key to a pair of handcuffs. They took it to Murray Police Department, where it opened the handcuffs removed from Carol DaRonch. Clearly the two cases were related. But while Carol had escaped, Debra had not.

The fact that both attacks had taken place on the same night in a supposedly safe area of the country attracted a great deal of attention. There were numerous phone calls to the police offering information. One man who had come to pick up his daughter after the play said he had seen an old, battered, light-coloured VW Beetle speeding out of the parking lot at around 10.30 pm that night.

Ten days after Debra's disappearance, Detective Ira Beal of the Bountiful Police Department got a call from the police in Park City, Utah, saying they had found a guy answering the description of the man they were looking for. He was a part-time drug dealer who worked in a local restaurant and drove a Volkswagen that belonged to his girlfriend. Detective Beal took Raelynne Shepard to Park City and they sat in the car outside the restaurant, waiting for the suspect to come to work.

When she saw him in the street Mrs Shepard could not be sure that he was the man she had seen at the play. However, inside, when he served them, she was convinced that it was. Naturally he denied it, and agreed to take a lie-detector test, which he passed with flying colours.

On the evening of his execution Bundy admitted killing Debra Kent and pointed out on a map where he had dumped her body, along with two of the other seven women he claimed to have killed in Utah. Months of searching afterwards resulted in the discovery of a single human patella. Belva Kent, along with her ex-husband Dean and two of their three surviving children, visited the rock-strewn hillside to take what solace they could find.

'I'm confident it's a good possibility that's where he disposed of the remains,' Dean Kent said. 'It's given me peace of mind to believe that's what happened.'

The state medical examiner said the patella was probably that of a young woman, but there was no way to determine if it was Debra Kent's.

After Debra disappeared her brother Bill, who idolized her, blamed himself. Ten years later, after his marriage had broken up, he died in an alcohol-related car accident, aged 26.

Within months of Bill's death Dean Kent started drinking, and then he walked out on his 29-year marriage. He quit his job and fathered another child, although he ended up living alone. He believed that Bundy was to blame.

'I certainly feel he was the cancer that destroyed our family,' he told the *Deseret News*.

The abduction of Debra Kent was tied by the media not just to the attack on Carol DaRonch, but also to the disappearance of Nancy Wilcox and the murders of Melissa Smith and Laura Aime. Clearly, a serial killer was at work.

Bundy read all the newspaper reports of his crimes and revelled in the fear that he spread among the people of Utah, just as he had in Washington State.

LIZ KENDALL CONTACTS THE POLICE

With abductions and killings now going on in Utah, Liz Kendall felt obliged to co-operate with the police in Washington State. After her initial calls, she agreed to meet King County Detective Randy Hergesheimer in the parking lot of the Herfy's restaurant that she and Bundy used to frequent.

She recognized the officer because he looked 'exactly like a detective sitting in a detective's unmarked car'.

Detective Hergesheimer said that they had already checked Bundy out. He had never been in trouble with the law and seemed to be clean in every way.

She pointed out that there was a side of Ted they did not know – he steals.

'I mean, he gets all dressed up in his fine clothes and then he shoplifts,' she said. 'He's taken everything from textbooks to a TV.'

She said she thought he enjoyed the 'con' of stealing, rather than the things he stole. And she told Hergesheimer about the

Ted Bundy in a 1975 Utah mug shot: Liz Kendall tried to bring Bundy to the attention of the police, but she had no conclusive evidence against him.

time she had accused Ted of being a thief and he told her, if she told anyone, he would 'break her f***ing neck.'

However, she had to admit that Ted did not usually have a violent temper. He had only hit her once, early on in their relationship. Liz had been drunk and had taunted him, saying: 'Go ahead and hit me. Go ahead.'

Eventually, he had slapped her. It had been in the parking lot at Herfy's.

Hergesheimer asked her if there was anything in Bundy's background that might affect how he felt about women. She said that Ted was illegitimate and his mother had never discussed it with him. Nevertheless, he was still close with her and with his half brothers and sisters.

Then Hergesheimer asked about their sex life. Liz said that it had been pretty good up until the previous summer, when he began to lose interest. She put this down to pressure of work and moving, though maybe he had another girlfriend. She didn't know.

She told Hergesheimer that Ted had bought a copy of *The Joy of Sex* in the autumn of 1973. They had read it together in bed.

'Ted sheepishly asked me if we could try bondage,' she said. 'We had sex that way maybe three times, but I didn't like it, so we stopped.'

As far as she knew, Bundy had not had any homosexual experiences, although during the past year he had talked about anal sex. But she did not like the idea of it.

Hergesheimer produced a list of the characteristics that a serial killer would possess. She found that Ted did not come close to the psychological profile outlined. One trait was that a killer would hate animals and have a history of being cruel to them. But Liz said Ted had taken in strays and plied her daughter Tina with kittens, hamsters and guinea pigs.

As a result of their conversation Detective Hergesheimer said that he pretty much ruled Bundy out of being the killer. Nevertheless, he asked Liz if she could provide some pictures of him which he could show to witnesses from Lake Sammamish Park. She was reluctant to do this, as it would be concrete proof that she had gone to the police and might be used against Ted if, as he said, he went on to pursue a political career.

Back at Liz's apartment, they went through her photograph albums. Detective Hergesheimer was impressed by how many shots showed Bundy with her or Tina. It was plain that they cared very much about each other.

Liz was relieved that Ted was not a suspect and felt guilty that she had suspected him. Her suspicions were further allayed when she discovered that Debra Kent had been abducted some time after 10 pm Pacific Standard Time on 8 November. Ted had called her at 11 pm, which would have been midnight in Utah. The call had been brief, but she thought it unlikely that he would have phoned if he had anything to do with the abduction. Liz had told him it was late and he should call her the next day. As it was, this gave him the rest of the night to toy with his victim.

That Christmas Liz returned to Utah to spend the holiday with Bundy and her parents. Again, he seemed perfectly normal and she could not believe that she had thought him a bloodthirsty murderer. By then they had been together for five years, and she was still determined to marry him.

But her doubts persisted. She told her father of her misgivings. He advised caution, lest she ruin Bundy's career. She also confided in her bishop, back in Seattle. Eventually she bit the bullet and called the Salt Lake City Homicide Department. She spoke to Captain Pete Hayward, who was heading the investigation in Utah. He said that his team had already checked Bundy out and found nothing. Liz now dreaded that one day Ted would find out that she had called the police about him.

CHAPTER FOUR
Colorado

AT THE BEGINNING of 1975 Bundy decided that he would buckle down to his studies. During his first year he had struggled to maintain a C average. He had been drinking a good deal and phoned Liz regularly, suspicious that she might be seeing someone else. He also decided that he had better move his murderous activities outside Utah. Killing again in the 'Beehive State' would prove too risky. A devoted skier, Bundy turned his eyes on Colorado.

CONFERENCE KILLING

That January a medical symposium on cardiology was being held in Aspen. Doctor Raymond Gadowski of Farming, Michigan, was attending and on 11 January he checked into the Wildwood Inn in nearby Snowmass, Colorado, with his fiancée, 23-year-old nurse Caryn Campbell, who was nine years his junior, and

Bundy helps a woman called Carol Bartholomew wash up after a birthday party in 1975. She later told a local newspaper she was disappointed he hadn't asked her out because she was convinced he would be a fun date.

two children from his first marriage, 11-year-old Gregory and 9-year-old Jenny.

Caryn had a mild case of flu, but managed to take the children skiing while Dr Gadowski attended seminars. That evening they ate at the Stew Pot with friends. Caryn ate a beef stew, but she was feeling a bit queasy so drank only milk, while the other adults had cocktails. Back in the lounge of the Wildwood Inn, Dr Gadowski picked up the evening paper. They were accompanied by a colleague who was a former boyfriend of Caryn's. He had a copy of *Playboy*. Caryn suggested he swap it for the latest issue of *Viva*, an adult magazine for women, which she had brought on the trip.

She asked Gadowski to go and get it. He refused, but handed her the key to their room, number 210. She got off the elevator on the second floor, where she spoke to a nurse from her hospital who was also attending the symposium. Then Caryn headed for her room.

Dr Gadowski expected her to return to the lounge within a few minutes. When she did not appear, he told the children to stay where they were in the lounge and set out to find her. He went up to the room and knocked on the door. He knocked again, in case she was in the bathroom. Again there was no response. Knowing she was ill, he was concerned that she had fainted inside.

He ran down to the front desk and got the passkey. When he entered the room, he saw Caryn's purse in the same place she had left it and the *Viva* still on the stand beside the bed. There were a number of parties going on that evening. Although she was not usually so inconsiderate as to take off without telling him, he checked the bars, but there was no sign of her. It had been a cold day and the temperature had dropped to −33°F after sunset. She had been wearing blue jeans and a light woolly jacket when she had headed for the elevator. It was inconceivable that she would have gone outside.

Snowmass is one of the most beautiful places in Colorado.

Dr Gadowski took the children up to the room. Soon after 10 pm, when Caryn still had not appeared, he called Aspen Police Department. Around 11 pm, a patrol car from Pitkin County Sheriff's Office arrived. The officers explained that almost everyone who had 'disappeared' turned up after the bars had closed and the parties had broken up. Gadowski insisted that Caryn was ill and he was concerned that her condition may have got worse.

The officers took a description, which was broadcast to other patrol cars in the area. During the night a number of young women were stopped. None of them turned out to be Caryn.

Michael Fisher, Chief Criminal Investigator for the Ninth Judicial District of the State of Colorado, was called in the next day. He was not particularly concerned at first. Alcohol had a greater effect at altitude and cocaine was plentiful in Aspen. It was not uncommon for people to go off with someone who was not their partner, or overdose and turn up in hospital.

If foul play was involved, Dr Gadowski and Caryn's former boyfriend were the most likely suspects. He interviewed them and quickly discounted them from the enquiry. Dr Gadowski and his two children stayed on at the Wildwood Inn for about a week before they flew home.

Meanwhile, detectives searched the building room by room, looking in closets, storerooms, even the kitchens, and peering down elevator shafts and up into crawlspaces. Caryn, they concluded, was not in the inn.

They questioned every guest. No one had seen her after she left the lift on the second floor. One woman from California named Elizabeth Harter had seen a handsome young man on the night of 12 January, who had smiled at her. She thought nothing of it and had left the inn before it became known that Caryn was missing.

If Caryn had been abducted, it was clear she had been taken out of the building without being seen. The inn was built in a U shape around a heated pool. The outdoor walkways to the rooms meant that normally the doors were clearly visible from other parts of the building. However, that night was particularly cold and the clouds of steam rising from the warm water rendered them invisible. Even so, it was clear to Colorado criminal investigator Michael Fisher that Caryn must have co-operated with her abductor, perhaps being lured away by some ruse.

Years later Bundy confessed to killing Caryn Campbell. He would not give details, other than to say that he had hit her over the head in his car, some way from the Wildwood Inn.

On 17 February a parks employee was working along Owl Creek, some 3 miles (5 km) from the Wildwood Inn when he noticed birds circling a snow bank 25 ft (8 m) from the road. He waded through a snowdrift and found the naked body of Caryn Campbell, frozen and half-eaten, lying on a patch of snow stained crimson with her blood. She was identified from her dental records. The cause of death was given as 'blows to the back of the head with a blunt object combined with exposure to sub-zero weather'. One of her teeth had been broken by the impact.

She had been killed soon after she had been taken, as the autopsy found beef stew and milk in her stomach. There was extensive damage to the soft tissue of her head and neck, and there were gnaw marks on the exposed flesh.

After the murder of Caryn Campbell, Bundy returned to Salt Lake City and got down to work. Others thought he must be a transfer student because he had so rarely attended class in the first semester. He soon gained a reputation for being able to pass tough courses while apparently doing little work. Nevertheless, he often appeared haggard, with bags under his eyes and scratches on his cheeks and neck. It seems likely that he was adding to the body count in Utah and the surrounding states.

A TERRIBLE SPRINGTIME REVELATION

The investigation in Washington State was getting nowhere. Then, as the snows receded that spring, Bundy's second dump site was found. Two students from Green River Community College were doing a survey of the forest on Taylor Mountain, Washington. On 1 March they stumbled across a skull, near where Highway 18 cut through the woodlands. The lower jaw was missing, but dental records showed it to be that of Brenda Ball. It was just 10 miles (16 km) from the hillside where the remains of Janice Ott and Denise Naslund were found. It was also only 30 miles (48 km) from the Flame Tavern, where Brenda had last been seen. Part of the right side of her cranium was also missing. The medical examiner said 'this [damage] was not caused by an animal'.

King County detective Bob Keppel led over 200 searchers, who scoured the area for eight days. They found no sign of the rest of Brenda's body, nor any of her clothes or personal effects. Even if animals had scattered her remains, something should have been found. What had happened to the bodies remains a mystery, but Bundy was always scrupulous when disposing of the clothes and other items that could carry hairs, fingerprints or other clues. These were usually thrown in a dumpster far from the deceased. As far as Bundy was concerned, the police could go on collecting bones as much as they liked. There was nothing to connect them to him.

What they did find in their search of Taylor Mountain, just 100 ft (30 m) away from Brenda's remains, was another skull. This belonged to Susan Rancourt, who had gone missing from Ellensburg 87 miles (140 km) away. Fifty feet further on, the search teams found another skull. Although all the upper teeth were missing, dental records confirmed that this belonged to

Kathy Parks, who had gone missing from Cornvallis, Oregon, 262 miles (420 km) away. Finally, the lower mandible of a human was found. Fillings in the remaining teeth matched those on Lynda Healy's dental charts.

It seemed as though the heads had been brought there one at a time over a period of six months. This led to rumours that the killings had something to do with cults, witchcraft or Satanism. Cult members contacted the police with reports that they had seen 'Ted' at meetings. A psychic contacted Captain Herb Swindler at the Seattle Police Department. She planted a stick in Taylor Mountain at dawn and tried to deduce something from its shadow, but no new theories were forthcoming.

By this point King County police had looked at 2,247 'Ted' lookalikes and checked out 916 vehicles. They had whittled down the list of possible suspects to 200. Bundy's name remained on the roster, but as he was a law student he seemed to be on the right side of the law. Records of his juvenile misdemeanours had been shredded.

A NEW HUNTING GROUND

By 14 March Bundy was on the move again. Later, his movements were tracked by his use of a Chevron credit card when he filled up with gas. He headed north into Wyoming, filling up at Rock Springs and Laramie. Then he turned south back into Colorado and on Saturday 15 March he drove into Vail.

Twenty-six-year-old Julie Cunningham lived in Vail, where she worked in a sports goods shop and shared an apartment with a friend. She was attractive and had her long dark hair parted in the middle. After a long phone call to her mother, she left her apartment at around 9 pm, wearing blue jeans, a brown suede jacket, boots and ski hat. She was heading for a tavern a few blocks away where her flatmate was waiting. Julie never arrived. When her flatmate returned to the apartment that evening, Julie was not there. Everything was just as she had left it and nothing was missing, apart from the clothes that Julie was wearing when she left.

Later, Bundy told Colorado investigator Michael Fisher what had happened. On the way to the bar Julie had seen Bundy on crutches, fumbling with some ski boots. He started to cross the street and asked for her help. He told her that he needed a little help to get into his car, which was parked a little way down the street in the direction she was going. They made small talk as they walked towards it.

He led her to the passenger door and asked her to help him by putting his crutches into the car. When he opened the door, she bent over. He hit her over the head and pushed her into the passenger seat. As he drove away he handcuffed the unconscious woman.

Turning off the Interstate 70 (I-70) highway on to a small local road, he drove to a small lake, then took a dirt road to a stand of juniper trees. On the way, Julie regained consciousness. Terrified, she begged for her life. This only turned him on.

Parking by the trees, he choked her until she passed out again, then had sex with her. He left the passenger door open, so that when she came to again, she would glimpse a chance to escape. She took it. But Bundy was only toying with her. He let her run for a short distance. There was no one for miles to hear her screams. Young and athletic, he chased her down and strangled her, leaving her naked body under a tree.

Her clothes were collected in a trash bag and thrown in a dumpster on the way back to Salt Lake City. Twice, Bundy made the 600-mile (966 km) round trip back to visit her body, burying what was left of it on the second occasion.

The second trip was on 3 April. For a couple of days he drove around Colorado. On Sunday 6 April he was travelling back on the I-70 through Grand Junction, which lies near the border with Utah. It was there that he spotted 24-year-old Denise Oliverson, who was slim with long brown hair parted in the middle.

That afternoon she had had an argument with her husband and she was riding her yellow ten-speed bicycle to her parents' home. It was a warm day and she was wearing jeans, sandals and a green printed, long-sleeved blouse. She was approaching a bridge that would take her over the Colorado River when Bundy pulled up in his Volkswagen and seized her.

With Denise now his prisoner, he continued westwards down the I-70. Before he reached the state line, he stopped, killed her, sexually abused her body and dumped it in the Colorado River. Her clothes and personal effects were dumped elsewhere.

She did not turn up at her parents' place that afternoon, but they had not been expecting her. Nor did she return home that evening. Her husband assumed she was staying with her parents. He would give her time to cool off before calling the following day. When he did, Denise's parents said that she had never arrived at their house. The police found her bike and her sandals under a viaduct near the Colorado River. The bike was in good working order. There was no reason to abandon it there. Denise's body was never found.

Back in Utah, Bundy dedicated himself to his academic work, not forgetting to send Liz flowers on her 30th birthday. To earn some money he worked as a custodian at Bailiff Hall in the University of Utah, a job he held for a couple of months until he was fired for missing work and turning up drunk.

In Colorado, criminal investigator Michael Fisher was still embroiled in the investigation of Caryn Campbell's murder. He tracked one suspect to Detroit, but after interviewing him there it was clear he wasn't the killer. While in Michigan, he interviewed Dr Raymond Gadowski and Caryn's ex again. They agreed to taking a polygraph test and passed. Dr Gadowski's 11-year-old son also substantiated their account.

INVESTIGATORS START TO CONNECT THE DOTS IN UTAH AND COLORADO

With the disappearance of Julie Cunningham and Denise Oliverson, Michael Fisher began to see a similar pattern to the one that had emerged in Utah, and he called Detective Jerry Thompson at Salt Lake City's Sheriff's Office to compare notes. They met up and it became clear that the murders in Utah and Colorado were the work of a single killer.

Eighteen-year-old Melanie Cooley could have been Debra Kent's twin, with her long brown hair parted in the middle. She was last seen hitchhiking home from her high school in Nederland, a mountain hamlet 50 miles (80 km) west of Denver, on 15 April. She was wearing blue jeans, a blue jean jacket with an embroidered eagle on the back and tan boots. Eight days later a road maintenance worker found her naked body on Coal Creek Canyon, 20 miles (32 km) away. She had been hit over the head repeatedly, possibly with a rock. Her hands were tied and she had a filthy pillowcase around her neck, which had possibly been used as a garrotte. Nederland was just 20 miles (32 km) from Golden, a small town Bundy had visited on 4 April, filling up with petrol there using his Chevron credit card.

CHAPTER FIVE
Madness

FOR HIS NEXT MURDER, Bundy strayed over the border into Idaho. On Monday 5 May 1975, he drove up the I-15 to Pocatello. He took a room in the Holiday Inn there, just a mile from Idaho State University. He signed in under a false name, although he gave the true registration number for his car.

Two days before Bundy's execution, Russell Reneau, Chief Investigator for the Idaho Attorney General's Office, asked him why he had visited Pocatello. He replied: 'It was madness ... It was basically to do what was done.'

At one point he admitted visiting the women's high-rise dormitory block at Idaho State University, but said he was confronted by a male security guard who asked him for ID. He was asked to leave. Dejected, he returned to his hotel room without a victim that day. The weather was unusually cold for May. There were snow flurries and few women were out walking on the street.

The following day it was still snowing, but Bundy got in his car and went out hunting. At lunchtime he saw a crowd of kids outside Alameda Junior High School, two miles (3 km) from his hotel. He got the attention of 12-year-old Lynette Culver, who lived across the street from the school. Although she was younger than his usual prey, she was 5 ft 2 in (157 cm) tall, weighing between 105–110 lb (48–50 kg) and had long brown hair parted down the middle. She wore jeans, a red checked shirt and a maroon jacket with a fur collar.

Bundy persuaded her to get into his car and chatted with her as he drove her back to the Holiday Inn. She told him that she was leaving the school grounds to meet someone for lunch. Other details Bundy recalled from their conversation checked out.

Bundy had taken a room on purpose at the rear of the hotel and no one saw Lynette enter the building with him. He drowned her in the bath in his room, then had sex with her dead body. He carried her body out to his Volkswagen, which was parked just 6 ft (1.8 m) from the rear door of the hotel, and put it in the trunk. Then he collected his luggage, drove north out of town and dumped her body in a river, leaving the residents of Pocatello to search fruitlessly for the 12-year-old.

Despite such horrendous crimes, Bundy managed to maintain the illusion of normality. When Liz Kendall returned home from work on 6 June, Tina asked her to come into her room.

'Suddenly, two arms slipped around me from behind,' Liz recalled. 'For a split second I froze in terror. It was Ted. My knees buckled and he had to hold me up.'

He stayed for almost a week. They went rafting together again. Everything was fine between them until Liz discovered that he was giving a woman and her 7-year-old son a lift back to Utah. Bundy insisted that the woman – the daughter of a Utah Supreme Court judge – was just a friend. This was not true. Her name was Leslie Knutson. For a while that summer they lived together and he played surrogate father to her son Josh. That did not stop Bundy going about his murderous business, though.

ATTACKS CONTINUE ACROSS STATE LINES

On 26 June 1975, 15-year-old Susan Curtis left her home in Bountiful, Utah, to cycle the 50 miles (80 km) to Provo with two female friends. They were attending a banquet on the campus of Brigham Young University as part of the Bountiful Orchard Youth Conference the next day and were staying with a friend.

Susan wore a yellow evening gown for the occasion. Her long brown hair was parted in the middle and she wore braces on her teeth. She needed to take care of them and told her companions that she was popping back to her room, which was about a quarter of a mile away, to clean her teeth. It was a warm summer evening, but it was already growing dark. She did not make it. Bundy had already had his head shaved to attach the electrode from the electric chair when he confessed to murdering Susan, and told prison superintendent Jim Barton where her body had been dumped. By grim coincidence, Susan Curtis had been to see *The Redhead* at Viewmont High School the night Debra Kent was snatched.

On 1 July Shelley Robertson did not turn up for work at her family's print business in Golden, Colorado. The family rang her boyfriend and other friends. She had last been seen on 30 June. Once she had been reported missing, a police office said he had seen her in a gas station with a wild-haired man driving a pickup. She had been hitchhiking. On 23 August her naked body was found 500 ft (152 m) inside a mine shaft by two mining students. She had been bound by duct tape. Her body was in such a bad state of decay that it was impossible to determine the cause of death. The mine shaft was near Vail, 60 miles (97 km) from Golden. It was searched thoroughly, in case Julie Cunningham's body had been dumped there too, but nothing more was found.

Twenty-three-year-old Nancy Baird went missing from the Fina gas station in Layton, 20 miles (32 km) north of Salt Lake City, on 4 July. It was 5.30 pm, the busiest part of the day, when she vanished from her work station, leaving behind her purse containing the money from her recently-cashed pay cheque. Her car was still in the parking lot where she had left it when she turned up to work. There were no signs of a struggle and nobody saw anything untoward. No trace of Nancy has ever been found.

Liz Kendall was back in Utah in late July. For her, this trip was a turning point. Either she and Ted were going to get married, or they would break up. On her first night the couple sat up late at her parents' kitchen table, drinking and talking. She asked him if he was still stealing. When he prevaricated, she exploded.

'You have a great future ahead of you and you jeopardize it with your stupid actions,' she said, accusing him of being a kleptomaniac. 'If you got caught stealing, I wouldn't stand by you for a second.'

The following day they went fishing in the Flaming Gorge National Recreational Area on the border with Wyoming. On the way home, they stopped at a beauty spot.

'Walking into the trees behind Ted, I was suddenly very scared and had an ominous feeling,' she said, turning and hurrying back to the car. 'Would I ever be normal again?' she wondered.

On the day she was to fly back to Seattle Liz delivered her ultimatum. To her surprise, he suggested that they get married at Christmas. But when she told her parents, the announcement was met with silence. Bundy was devastated. He thought they liked him. Although she had confided her suspicions to her dad earlier, Liz had recently reassured him that both the King County and Salt Lake City police had checked Bundy out and found nothing. When she returned to Seattle and handed in her notice, her boss told her that he thought she was making a mistake marrying Bundy. Her friend Angie, who also had doubts about Bundy, thought it was a mistake too. Liz was upset that no one was happy for her.

She then discovered that Bundy had been stealing again. She thought she had made it clear that he had to choose between theft and her, and called Ted to break off their relationship. He appeared relieved. Then she bumped into his former landlady, who told her that the police were making enquiries about Bundy again. Liz called King County Police, who then told her that Bundy had been arrested.

FORTUITOUS ARREST

On the night of 15 August 1975 Bundy was driving around Salt Lake County, smoking dope. He claimed that he was not hunting for a fresh victim, but it was clear that if he had seen a young woman hitchhiking he would have stopped for her. Around 2.30 am on 16 August he was sitting in his car in a side road in Granger, Utah, smoking a joint and studying a map, when he was suddenly dazzled by the headlights of a patrol car. Bundy panicked and took off at speed, neglecting to turn his headlights on. Sergeant Bob Hayward of the Utah Highway Patrol followed him as he ran two stop signs. He was, coincidentally, the brother of Captain Pete Hayward, who was heading the homicide investigation in Utah out of Salt Lake City. When Bundy hit the main road, he flicked his lights on, but Sergeant Hayward continued the chase. There had been a series of burglaries in the area and Sergeant Hayward thought he was pursuing one of the thieves.

Unable to shake the patrol car, Bundy threw the dope out of the window and pulled into a derelict gas station. Sergeant Hayward was calling for backup when the driver got out. He had fuzzy shoulder-length hair and was wearing blue jeans, a black turtleneck sweater and tennis shoes. Walking to the rear of the car, he smiled and said: 'I guess I am lost.'

Keeping his hand on his .38, Sergeant Hayward said: 'You ran two stop signs.' He asked to see Bundy's licence and registration information. Bundy got them from his car and Sergeant Hayward studied them.

'What are you doing out here at this time of the morning?' he asked.

Bundy said he had been to see *The Towering Inferno* at the Redwood drive-in nearby. The cinema was in Sergeant Hayward's patrol area. He had driven past it earlier that night and knew that *The Towering Inferno* was not playing there.

When two more troopers from the Highway Patrol pulled up, Sergeant Hayward asked to look in Bundy's car.

'Go ahead,' Bundy said.

The first thing he noticed was that the passenger seat had been removed and lay on its side on the back seat. Then he noticed a small crowbar lying on the floor behind the driver's seat. The beam from his flashlight played over a brown gym bag in the well where the passenger seat had been. It was open and Hayward could see some of the contents – rope, wire, an ice pick and a ski mask. These were part of Bundy's murder kit, but to Sergeant Hayward they looked like the tools of the trade of a burglar.

Sergeant Hayward arrested Bundy for evading an officer, frisked and handcuffed him. Then he called Salt Lake County Sheriff's Office, asking them to send a detective. When Detective Darrell Ondrak arrived on the scene, he found Bundy in the custody of Sergeant Hayward, Sergeant John Fife and Deputy Steven Twitchell. Detective Ondrak and Sergeant Hayward said that Bundy gave them permission to search his car. Bundy denied this.

'I never said: "Yes, you have my permission to search",' he maintained, 'but I was surrounded by a number of uniformed men: Sergeant Hayward, two highway patrolmen, two uniformed deputies. I wasn't exactly quaking in my boots, but I felt I couldn't stop them. They were intent and hostile, and they'd do what they damn well pleased.'

According to the arrest report, when Detective Ondrak examined the contents of the gym bag he found: 'One nylon white rope approximately 7 ft [2 m] in length. One tan with dark brown stripe ski mask. One brown cotton glove with leather hand grip. One Sears model 6577 pry bar. One black leather ski glove. One pair of panty hose with eye and nose holes cut out. One box of Glad trash bags. One Eveready Captains brand flashlight. One piece of orange wire four feet [120 cm] in length. One ice pick with a red handle. Eight strips of white sheet material cloth [of] different lengths.' A pair of handcuffs was also found in the trunk.

'Where did you get this stuff?' Detective Ondrak asked Bundy.

'It's just junk I picked up around the house,' Bundy said.

'They look like burglar tools to me,' said Detective Ondrak. 'I'm going to take these items, and I suspect the DA [District Attorney] will be issuing a charge of possession of burglar tools.'

Bundy replied simply: 'Fine.'

He was then taken to the police station, booked and photographed. Before he was bailed on his own recognizance, that is, without bail; that morning, he came face to face with Detective Jerry Thompson, who was investigating the Utah murders. Neither realized the significance of this meeting.

However, it began to dawn on Detective Thompson the following Monday, when he was glancing through the arrest reports for the weekend and came across the name 'Bundy'. He had heard that name before and remembered the young woman from Seattle who had made enquiries about a Ted Bundy the previous December.

The handcuffs found in the trunk reminded him of the attack on Carol DaRonch. She had also been threatened with an iron bar similar to the crowbar found in Bundy's car. He had also been arrested in Granger, just a few miles from where Melissa Smith was last seen alive.

His suspicions were reinforced by Detective Ondrak, who brought up Bundy's arrest at a meeting of detectives from surrounding counties and departments.

'I thought for a while Bundy was an armed robber, but we didn't find a weapon,' he told the others. 'He's not just your ordinary prowler. Some of the stuff we found in his car is obviously for tying someone up. I don't know. Bundy is the strangest man I ever met.'

Detective Thompson asked Detective Ondrak what he meant by that.

'I used to be in the Marine Corps,' said Detective Ondrak. 'You meet a lot of strange people in the Corps. I don't know. It's just a gut reaction. This man's into something big.'

'MY GAME IS HOMICIDE'

After the meeting Detective Thompson got on the phone to Detective Bob Keppel in Seattle. They began to suspect that they had got their man. In the meantime they had a charge they could hold him on. On 21 August Bundy was formally arrested for the possession of burglary tools. Bundy was sanguine. It was only a misdemeanour.

At the police station Bundy was asked about the things found in his car. He said he had found the handcuffs in a dumpster. The panty hose with the eye holes and the legs knotted on top was worn under the ski mask to protect him from the icy winds on the slopes. He seemed faintly amused when asked about the crowbar, ice pick and garbage bags. Didn't everyone own such things? How could they be deemed burglary tools?

Detective Thompson's partner, Detective Ben Forbes, then intimated that the situation was much more serious.

'My game is homicide,' he said.

Bundy said nothing. Nevertheless, he signed a form consenting to the search of his apartment. Detective Thompson accompanied Bundy to his second floor flat, less than a mile from the police station. The place was clean and tidy, but Detective Thompson's eye quickly fell on a pair of patent leather shoes like those Carol DaRonch and Raelynne Shepard had mentioned. Later, when Detective Thompson returned to the flat, the shoes were gone. The stereo and the TV had also been removed.

Bundy remained jovial and self-confident during the search, during which detectives found ski maps of Colorado with the Wildwood Inn marked, and a brochure from the Bountiful Recreation Center in Utah. Bundy said he had never been to Colorado. This was easily disproved by the copy of a Chevron petrol bill and a phone bill that listed a call from Denver. A friend must have left the maps there, he said. He also feigned ignorance of Bountiful, asking whether it was a city just north of Salt Lake City and saying he might have driven through it.

The brochure carried an advertisement for *The Redhead* at Viewmont High in Bountiful. Again, a friend or one of their children had left it there, he said. But that was the only evidence the detectives unearthed. They found no women's clothes, purses or jewellery, as they had hoped they would – nothing to tie Bundy to any of his victims.

After the search was completed Bundy gave them permission to photograph his car. It was parked around the back of the building. Bundy then returned to the police station with them, but made bail by morning. He agreed to return for further questioning. Instead, Bundy's new-found attorney John O'Connell turned up for the appointment wearing a cowboy hat and boots, telling the police that he had instructed his client not to talk to them – certainly not about 'the murder of all these girls'.

Detective Thompson called criminal investigator Michael Fisher in Colorado and told him about the map with the Wildwood Inn marked out.

'That's the place where our girl went out,' Fisher exclaimed. But it worried him that, if Bundy had been responsible for Caryn Campbell's murder, why would he hold onto anything that could connect him with the crime scene? Nevertheless, Fisher took down the number of Bundy's Chevron card, so he could check whether he had bought any gas in Colorado.

The police interviewed Leslie Knutson, who told them that sex between her and Bundy was normal. However, her ex-husband told the police that Bundy was always cleaning out his car, taking out the seats and vacuuming it. He asked himself: 'Why would anyone clean a ratty Volkswagen so often?'

By then Bundy was drinking heavily again and frequently telephoning Liz Kendall, blurting out one evening that his world was 'falling apart'. He now had a problem. Under close surveillance, he had no outlet for his murderous cravings.

WITNESSES START TO IDENTIFY BUNDY

Detective Thompson showed the pictures of Bundy's Volkswagen Beetle and his mug shot among a selection of others to Carol DaRonch. She picked out Bundy's photograph, saying that he looked a lot like the man who had attacked her, but she couldn't be sure. Raelynne Shepard also said that the photo of Bundy looked a lot like the man she had seen the night Debra Kent went missing, if you added a moustache. Then Fisher phoned Detective Thompson to tell him that not only had Bundy been in Colorado, but he had also filled up with petrol nearby where the women had gone missing. They were now convinced that they had got their man.

Detective Thompson also took out a subpoena to obtain Bundy's phone records, bank statements and schedules and grades from law school. When he went to pick up the details from the University of Utah, he was confronted by Bundy, who said: 'Jerry, you're grasping at straws.'

Investigator Fisher and Detective Thompson were also in regular communication with Detective Bob Keppel in Seattle. All three were now determined to build a watertight case against

Bundy. Detective Thompson took detectives Ira Beal and Ron Ballantyne from Bountiful Police Department in Utah when he visited Bundy in his apartment again, this time to serve a subpoena for an appearance in an identity parade.

'Oh, is that all?' said Bundy, visibly relieved.

After they had left, Bundy went to have his long hair shorn and parted it on the other side. Nevertheless, Carol DaRonch, Raelynne Shepard and Tamra Tingey, a school friend of Debra Kent who had also seen Bundy on the night she went missing, all picked him out. Bundy was shocked when his lawyer O'Connell told him.

Mugshots of Bundy were sent to Fisher in Colorado and, when the witness Elizabeth Harter returned to the Wildwood Inn the following year, she too picked him out.

She told Fisher that she remembered him because he was 'strange'. While everyone else was dressed for skiing or wearing warm clothing, he was wearing light trousers with no scarf, gloves or boots.

SERIOUS CHARGES AND SURVEILLANCE IN SEATTLE

On 2 October 1975 Bundy was charged with the kidnapping and attempted murder of Carol DaRonch in Murray, Utah. Bail was set at $100,000, the equivalent of $470,000 today.

After he had spent two weeks in jail, it was reduced to $15,000 ($70,000 today). His mother and stepfather raised the bond. Then, when he came out of jail, the story broke in the media. People who knew him were aghast.

Liz Kendall was stunned when Detective Thompson called to give her the news. She got drunk and sought comfort from the father of her daughter Tina and his fiancée. She also talked to Ted's mother. 'She seemed to be taking it better than I was,' Liz said, 'but she hadn't betrayed him.'

The Seattle newspapers speculated that the 'Ted' arrested in Utah was also the 'Ted' who was wanted in Washington. Bundy wrote to Liz. She did not write back.

'What could I say?' she said. '"Dear Ted. Hope you're enjoying jail. I helped put you there. Love, Liz".'

When he phoned, she told him about her conversations with King County and Salt Lake City police.

'It's okay. You did what you had to do,' he said. 'If you told them the truth, then no harm has been done because the truth is good enough. The truth will prove me innocent.'

Although he had been told not to talk to the police, Bundy also phoned Detective Jerry Thompson, protesting his innocence. Then Detective Thompson had a call of his own to make. On 10 November he phoned King County police to tell them that Bundy had made bail with no restrictions on his travel. Clearly, it was likely that he would travel to Seattle.

There were still plenty of people in Seattle who knew Bundy and believed he was innocent. They were happy to contribute to his defence fund. Liz was terrified that Bundy would turn up and asked the police to contact her as soon as he crossed the state line. Nevertheless, once he was back in Seattle, he managed to persuade Liz to let him stay with her and to stop co-operating with the police.

Law enforcement's major problem was making sure that Bundy did not kill again. This meant 24-hour surveillance.

In response, he tailed the officers who were following him, noting their licence plate numbers and taking their photographs. He took great pleasure in giving them the slip, but was unfailingly courteous, even inviting a detective in on one occasion. He was asked to leave, once Bundy got his attorney on the phone.

On 1 December 1975 the alarm bells rang when Bundy was spotted on the campus of the University of Washington in Seattle. He went back there again the following day and was asked to leave. He also had lunch with Ann Rule that day. They had not seen each other for two years. She paid the bill.

'When all this is over,' he said, 'I will take you out to lunch.'

Ann found that she could not cross-examine him, but was prepared to listen to what he had to say.

'He continued to toss away the Utah charges as if they were no more important than a slight misunderstanding,' she said. 'He was supremely confident that he would win in court in the DaRonch case; the burglary tools charges were too ridiculous to discuss.'

Finally, she asked him about the women who had gone missing in Washington State. He denied even reading about them in the newspapers. But he could not meet her gaze and she knew that he was lying.

They met again on 17 January 1976 in a tavern. Ann asked Bundy: 'Do you like women?'

'Yes,' he said. 'I think I do.'

He even told her that Liz had reported him to the police, telling them about the crutches and plaster of Paris she had seen in his room. Ann told him that she had a contract to write a book about the missing girls and women, and warned him: 'I cannot be completely convinced of your innocence.'

When she returned from the ladies' room, Bundy sneaked up behind her and grabbed her around the waist. It appeared that he liked sneaking up on women. He also lied to her when he said that he had never phoned her from Utah. She had the telephone records to prove it.

After chatting for nearly six hours, Ann had to go, although she felt that Bundy had more he wanted to tell her. He was quite drunk and said he was going to smoke a joint. They hugged and parted.

CHAPTER SIX
Days in Court

DETECTIVES in Utah, Colorado and Washington State were convinced that Ted Bundy was a depraved serial killer, but they did not have the evidence to prove it. Their only hope of getting him off the streets so he could not kill again was to have him convicted for the kidnapping of Carol DaRonch, because by now the attempted murder charges had been dropped.

The trial began on Monday 23 February 1976 in Salt Lake City and would last a week. *The New York Times* said: 'Those who saw him for the first time agreed with those who had known him for all his 28 years: there must have been some terrible mistake. Here was a young man who represented the best in America, not its worst. Here was this terrific-looking man with light brown hair and blue eyes, looking rather Kennedyesque, dressed in a beige turtleneck and dark blue blazer, a smile turning the corners of his lean all-American face, walking almost jauntily before the judge, but free of any extravagant motion that could lead one to think a swaggering – even dangerous – personality existed beneath that casual, cool exterior.'

It was noticed that he was very relaxed, as you would expect of a young man who had two years' experience of law school. At the defence table he was seen reading a copy of Aleksandr Solzhenitsyn's *The Gulag Archipelago*, first published in English that year.

He joked with local reporters that the eight weeks he had spent in jail in Salt Lake City before being given bail was useful experience for someone studying law and had given him ideas on how to improve the system.

'We can start with the bail-bond system,' he said.

The trial was welcome, he told reporters.

'I want to clear my name,' he said. 'I want it all out in the open. I want it aired.'

Bundy's attorney John O'Connell opted for a bench trial – that is, a hearing without a jury where Bundy's guilt or innocence would be decided solely by Judge Stewart M. Hanson. They were confident that the judge would decide the case purely on the law, while a jury was more likely to be swayed by public opinion.

The key witness was Carol DaRonch herself. She was unsettled in court by Bundy, who stared fixedly at her, and she frequently sobbed during her testimony. Crucially, she identified Bundy as the man who had introduced himself to her as 'Officer Roseland'. O'Connell cross-examined the weeping Carol for two hours, suggesting that she had been coerced by the police into pointing the finger at Bundy.

'You identified pretty much what the law enforcement officers wanted you to, didn't you?' he suggested.

'No ... no,' she replied softly.

He rattled her with a question about the colour of the badge she had been shown on the night of the incident. Was it gold or silver? Bundy had flashed it at her. She had glimpsed it for a split second 16 months before and was reduced to waffling. Nevertheless, she was clear on the crucial details of the incident.

When he tried to handcuff her, she said: 'I was screaming, asking him what he was doing. Then he pulled a gun, a small black one, and said he would blow my brains out. I got out the door and he slid across the seat after me. I was screaming as loud as I could and scratching him.'

She admitted being hysterical at the time. Some of her testimony contradicted her earlier identification of Bundy's car. She also admitted that she had not been able to make a positive identification of Bundy from a photograph and could not even say whether her assailant had a moustache or not. Even so, Judge Hanson found her testimony credible.

Wilbur and Mary Walsh, who had picked her up after the attack, also testified. Defence attorney O'Connell tried to have the testimony of Sergeant Bob Hayward concerning the night of Bundy's arrest suppressed, but failed.

The grieving Kent family sat in the courtroom. They still did not have Debra Kent's body to lay to rest. Police chief Louis Smith of Midvale in Salt Lake City was also there. He believed that Bundy was responsible for the abduction and murder of his daughter Melissa. O'Connell was afraid that Smith might have brought his service revolver with him and asked Assistant County Prosecutor David Yocom to go out into the crowded courtroom to check. After that, guards frisked him every day.

Bundy's mother and stepfather were there too. Liz Kendall took the week off to attend, even though Bundy asked her not to come. His attorney feared that she might be called as a witness for the prosecution. Liz was relieved that Leslie Knutson would not be there.

Bundy himself took the stand. He admitted lying to Sergeant Hayward after being apprehended. He had fled from the police, he said, because he had been smoking marijuana. He wanted to throw the joint out of the car and let the smoke clear. He also admitted that he had not been to the drive-in cinema that night, as he had said.

He had no clear alibi for the night of 8 November, but denied ever seeing Carol DaRonch before she came into court. He claimed he had picked up the handcuffs found in his car at a dump and had kept them as a curio. He had no key for them.

'Have you ever worn a false moustache?' asked Prosecutor Yocom during his cross-examination. 'Didn't you wear one when you were a spy in the [Governor] Dan Evans campaign?'

'I wasn't spying for anyone,' said Bundy, 'and I never wore a false moustache during that period.'

'Didn't you brag to a woman acquaintance that you like virgins and you can have them at any time?' Yocom continued.

'No,' said Bundy.

'Didn't you tell that same woman that you saw no difference between right and wrong?'

'I don't remember that statement. If I made it, it was taken out of context and does not represent my views.'

'Did you ever use an old licence plate on your car after you'd received new plates from the state of Utah?'

'No sir.'

'You notified the state that you had lost plates bearing the numbers LJE-379 on 11 April 1975. These slips show that you were still using those "lost" plates in the summer of 1975. Why was that?'

'I cannot remember the incidents,' said Bundy. 'The attendant probably asked for my plate numbers and I may have inadvertently given him the old numbers from memory.'

Bundy had been caught out in a series of lies. They were small ones that might have been dismissed by a jury, but they damaged his plausibility in the eyes of Judge Hanson.

On Thursday night, after Ted had finished testifying, Liz Kendall flew to Salt Lake City. Bundy met her at the airport.

'Ted looked handsome and his spirits were high,' she said.

They had dinner in a Mexican restaurant. Back at his place, they agreed that she should not attend court the following morning. However, when she had just stepped out of the shower, the phone rang and she was told to come as quickly as possible. Ted wanted her there.

When she arrived, Bundy turned and smiled at her. David Yocom was making his closing arguments and said that all the descriptions of the assailant fitted Bundy to a T. He then pulled out a chair and sat down. Pretending to be Bundy in the front seat of his car, he demonstrated to the judge how Bundy had tried to put the handcuffs on Carol DaRonch.

Judge Hanson then made his summing up. He would take the weekend to decide his verdict.

Bundy spent most of the weekend with Liz. He expressed his fear of going to jail.

'If I can't be free, I want to be dead,' he said.

Liz thought maybe he should take the car and flee to Mexico. Instead, they got drunk and doped themselves with Valium and marijuana, distracting themselves by watching *Monty Python*, which Liz did not understand, and *Saturday Night Live*. Liz had Sunday lunch with her parents. The conversation was strained because they could not understand why she was still standing by him. She finished the day with Ted, making love.

They tried to do it again the following morning, thinking it might be the last time, but their nerves got the better of them.

'I love you so much,' he said. She started to cry.

O'Connell called at 9 am, telling Bundy to get to his office. Judge Hanson had reached a verdict. Liz dropped him off and went to find a parking place. She said she would meet him in the judge's chambers, where she found Judge Hanson talking to Bundy's mother. When Ted came in he gave Liz a wink and a forced smile.

In the courtroom Bundy fiddled nervously with his hair. Captain Pete Hayward and Detective Jerry Thompson were there. Judge Hanson said that after agonizing over his verdict during the weekend, he found Bundy guilty of aggravated kidnap beyond reasonable doubt. Bundy was then remanded in custody prior to sentencing.

Bundy asked for a few moments alone with his family. But Captain Hayward and Detective Thompson seized him, put his arms behind his back and handcuffed him.

'You don't need those,' said Bundy through clenched teeth. 'I'm not going anywhere.'

Liz was distraught.

'They were going to take him because of all the garbage I had told them,' she said. 'I had tried to tell them I was wrong, but they wouldn't listen. They were so desperate to solve their cases that they had taken a man who might be a thief and had made him a mass murderer.'

She leaned close to Detective Thompson and said: 'Revenge is sweet, isn't it, Jerry?'

'I wanted to spit in his face, claw his eyes out, hammer him,' she recalled.

She put her arms around Bundy and told him that she loved him. He did not respond.

'Let's go,' said the detectives. 'Take him downstairs.'

DETECTIVES EXAMINE THE INFAMOUS VW BEETLE

While Bundy languished in Salt Lake County Jail, the murder investigations in Utah, Colorado and Washington State continued. Although he had sold his VW Beetle in the autumn of 1975, the police retrieved it. Colorado criminal investigator Michael Fisher wanted to examine it and got permission from the Salt Lake County Sheriff's Office to transport it there.

First he tracked down the young man who had purchased it. Investigator Fisher asked him what he had done in the car that might contaminate the evidence and took some hair samples from him. Then he set about finding out what the Salt Lake forensic examiners had done. While they had removed the seats and taken up the floor mats, he discovered that the roof lining and interior door panels had not been removed.

He picked up the car in a rental truck and transported it to the Colorado Bureau of Investigation in Denver. There they stripped the car down, finding more hairs behind the back seat. Then they took the door-side panels out. On the passenger-side window, below the weatherproof seal, they found blood. It had run down between the glass and the felt that seals the inside of the door. Samples were taken and photographed, and more hairs were found.

Back in Salt Lake City, Bundy was undergoing psychological evaluation before sentencing. Doctor Al Carlisle, a clinical psychologist on the medical staff at Utah State Prison, liked Bundy, although he recognized him as a sociopath. Revealingly, Bundy asked Dr Carlisle whether he thought he was responsible for the Washington State murders. Dr Carlisle was noncommittal, afraid that any comment would taint his findings.

The constant theme running through Bundy's psychiatric assessments was that he viewed women as being more competent than men. According to Carlisle: 'There were indications of a fairly strong dependency on women, and yet he also has a strong need to be independent. I feel this creates a fairly strong conflict, in that he would like a close relationship with females but is fearful of being hurt by them. There were indications of general anger and, more particularly, well-masked anger toward women.'

Although Bundy appeared to have had a normal childhood, on closer study it was clear that he was a classic loner. When the psychiatrist carrying out the evaluation of him in the Utah prison enquired why he had not broadened his social activities at junior high school, as his friends were doing at that time, Bundy said that he felt 'apprehension toward establishing new relationships,' and that he was 'just as secure with the academic life.'

He went to parties, engaged in some kissing and petting, but he did not date until his senior year at high school.

'He indicated that while in the 12th grade, his "social deficits were cured", he had "neutral feelings about girls" and he indicated he had no inhibitions or fears, but just a lack of motivation toward dating,' the psychiatrist's report said.

In college, he 'had a longing for a beautiful co-ed but "I didn't have the skill or social acumen to cope with it."' He studied Chinese to 'gain a position of authority to improve the relationships between the US and China', but later changed to urban studies to help change the plight of the poor, he told friends. He met a young woman from a wealthy San Francisco family who was his first 'real involvement', but felt quite insecure in the relationship and said they were 'worlds apart'.

CHAPTER SIX

Bundy also consented to see Investigator Michael Fisher. Bundy's defence attorney O'Connell was against the interview and insisted that Fisher tell him what he would be questioning his client about. Investigator Fisher said he wanted to talk about the murder of Caryn Campbell. Bundy was evasive, saying he could not remember whether he was in Colorado on the night in question. However, Investigator Fisher had a receipt from a gas station, signed by Bundy, in Glenwood Springs, less that 40 miles (64 km) from Aspen, Colorado. When pressed, Bundy said that he had been out driving to relieve the pressure of studying for his forthcoming law exams.

Towards the end of the interview Investigator Fisher asked him directly whether he had killed a young woman on the trip to Aspen.

'I certainly didn't kill anyone anywhere,' Bundy insisted. 'Wherever it was, I didn't kill anyone.'

Investigator Fisher did more investigation in Utah, hoping to shore up his Caryn Campbell case with 'similar transactions' – that is, occasions outside his jurisdiction where the suspect had exhibited the same criminal behaviours. He also had good physical evidence. Hairs found in Bundy's VW Beetle by Colorado Bureau of Investigation forensics matched those, not just of Caryn Campbell, but also of Carol DaRonch and Melissa Smith.

Bundy returned to court for sentencing on 30 June. In tears, he complained of the injustice being done to him. Despite the verdict he continued to insist he was innocent. Nevertheless, Judge Hanson sentenced him to one to 15 years in prison.

However, Bundy was determined this would not be the end of his murderous career. On 19 October a prison warden found him hiding behind a bush in the prison yard with an escape kit comprising a social security card, a sketch of a driver's licence, road maps and details of airline schedules. He was given 15 days in solitary confinement.

In October 1976 an arrest warrant for Bundy was signed in Colorado for the murder of Caryn Campbell. He did not fight extradition, hinting that he had documents that would destroy the case against him. 'The Colorado trial will mark the beginning of the end of a myth,' he told Ann Rule.

Investigator Fisher came to collect him from Utah State Prison early in the morning of 28 January 1977 at around 4 am. This was done to minimize the chances of any family member of Bundy's victims administering their own summary justice. Bundy himself was afraid that the cops might take the opportunity to kill him as they drove him back to Colorado. He even slid down on to the floor when a speeding car caught up with their unmarked vehicle.

On the way, they drove through Grand Junction, where Denise Oliverson had gone missing. Asked if the place looked familiar, Bundy refused to speak. Indeed, he kept silent until he was delivered safely to Pitkin County Courthouse in Aspen. The jail there was nearly a century old and generally held drunks and petty criminals. A new health ordinance prohibited prisoners being kept there for more than 30 days, so Bundy was transferred to Garfield County Jail in Glenwood Springs, an hour's drive away.

THE FIRST JAIL BREAK AND RECAPTURE

With his jailers, Bundy ladled on the charm, hoping they would drop their guard. Judge George Lohr was also taken in. After Wildwood Inn guest and witness Elizabeth Harter

Ted Bundy is led into the Pitkin County courthouse by police officers for a hearing in Aspen, Colorado. But he wasn't that well guarded. Bundy was charged with murder, but jumped out of a second-story window and escaped during a court recess.

failed to identify Bundy at a pre-trial hearing, he granted Bundy permission to use the courthouse's law library as he was conducting his own defence. He was also given permission to appear in court without shackles.

On 7 June 1977 Bundy dressed himself in several layers of clothing. It was early summer and warm during the day, but at night it was freezing due to the altitude. During the mid-morning recess, Bundy retired to the law library upstairs. A window had been left open to let fresh air into the stuffy room.

Alone there, Bundy looked out of the window. When the coast was clear he climbed out onto the window ledge and jumped. He ran across the courthouse lawn and over the street, climbed a fence and disappeared down an alleyway.

At the outskirts of the town he hid in the gorge of the Roaring Fork River. There, he stripped off his outer layers of clothing, leaving only a pair of running shorts and vest. Then he tied a red bandana around his head and tied the rest of his clothes up in a bundle.

His plan was to climb Aspen mountain, which was over 10,000 ft (3,048 m) high, and reach Crested Butte on the other side, nearly 25 miles (40 km) away. It was rough terrain and Bundy got lost. For five days he wandered through the cold and rain. Eventually he found shelter, breaking into an empty cabin. After a night's sleep, he ate what little food had been left there. It also provided a .22 rifle and bullets, some blankets, a torch and a first aid kit. Taking those, he headed off again.

When Bundy had made his break, Investigator Michael Fisher was in hospital having surgery on his knee. He discharged himself, furious because he had warned Bundy's jailers that he might escape. A clerk in the courthouse had also voiced her suspicions.

Bundy had injured himself jumping from the window. His leg began to swell up. During his time in the mountains he lost weight as he dodged the helicopters sent out to pursue him. From the footprints in the snow it was easy to spot the cabin he was staying in. He also ran into a local landowner, who toted a gun and warned him to watch out. A manhunt for the notorious Ted Bundy was going on in the area.

On the evening of his fifth day on the run, Bundy stumbled back into Aspen. Realizing that he was not going to be able to escape on foot, he decided to steal a car. He found a Cadillac with its doors left open. The ignition keys were under the front seat. Heading east out of Aspen towards Denver, he found the road was blocked by an avalanche. At 2 am the following morning, a patrol car sent out to investigate an assault and possible rape spotted a blue Cadillac weaving down the highway. Bundy was not a good driver and had little practice handling a large car. The police officers suspected that the man behind the wheel might be drunk and pulled him over. Shining a flashlight in his face, they immediately recognized him as the fugitive the police were scouring the countryside for.

Once Bundy was back in jail, none of the court-appointed attorneys could help him as they were witnesses to his escape and could be called in subsequent proceedings. John Browne, an attorney from Seattle, gave him some advice and Judge Lohr again cut him some slack, ruling out any of Investigator Fisher's investigations in Utah as 'similar transactions'. But now Bundy had to wear chains and leg irons in court.

He also wanted to change the venue for the trial, as Bundy was now too well known in Aspen. Judge Lohr agreed and sent the case to El Paso County, whose county seat was Colorado Springs. This did not work in Bundy's favour, as it was the jurisdiction that boasted the highest number of men sentenced to die in the gas chamber. The order came just before Christmas – 'My Christmas present from the court,' Bundy told a friend on the phone, 'a guaranteed death sentence.'

This meant that Bundy would be moved from Garfield County Jail, which he had already been assessing for its escape

Police and trained scent dogs search outlying areas for traces of Ted Bundy. Aspen residents complained about the fugitive's escape, accusing the police of being 'patently naïve and bordering on the criminally stupid'.

Captured: wearing a torn prison uniform and looking weary, Ted Bundy returned to Pitkin County court to resume hearings over his death penalty.

potential, to El Paso County Jail, where the regime was far more stringent. He had to move fast.

In Garfield County Jail his cell had a loose light fitting. A fellow inmate had given him a small hacksaw blade which he used to cut through the welds so he could remove the fixture completely. This gave him access to the crawl space above the ceiling. He was heard by other prisoners exploring the space above their heads. They reported this to the warders, who did nothing.

Bundy heard that Liz Kendall was thinking of marrying another man, so he began writing to Carole Boone, a woman he had known from Seattle. She believed in his innocence and began sending him packages of health food. Then she came to visit him. Although he ruthlessly destroyed the women who became his victims, he still craved intimacy with the opposite sex and the appearance of normality, as well as using women for financial support.

AN INGENIOUS ESCAPE ATTEMPT SUCCEEDS

On 30 December 1977 Bundy told the guards that he was not feeling well. With law books, clothes and other things to hand, he shaped what looked like a body under the blanket, then he took out the light fitting and the ceiling panel it was attached to and hauled himself up into the crawl space.

Bundy had already discovered that, beyond the cells, the crawl space led to the ceiling above an apartment occupied by the head jailer and his wife. That night, he heard, they were going to the movies. Bundy seized the opportunity. He crawled across the ceiling, dropped down into their apartment and changed his prison uniform for civilian clothing he found in a wardrobe there.

Outside it was snowing. Bundy braved the cold and searched for a car to steal. However, the one he found quickly packed up. So he took a Greyhound bus to Denver, where he boarded a plane for Chicago. He had $700 on him, which had been given to him as donations to his defence fund. It would be 17 hours before anyone in Garfield County Jail realized he was gone. Investigator Fisher was livid as, once again, he had warned of a potential escape.

From Chicago Bundy took a train to Ann Arbor, Michigan, where he checked into the YMCA. There he heard the first reports of his jailbreak, but neither the staff or fellow residents put two and two together. He was surprised that news of his escape was being carried as far away as Michigan, but it did not worry him. It was clear from the report that no one knew where he was. To the authorities, though, his escape was tantamount to a confession of murder. Now, once more, they had a serial killer on the loose.

CHAPTER SEVEN
Tallahassee

IN PREPARATION for his escape, Bundy had grown a beard and let his hair grow long again. Now he shaved and had his hair cut short. Passing himself off as a medical student, he went to a college bar. He drank beer while watching a college football game and got so drunk that he spent the second half retching in the men's room, until the bartender threatened to call the police and have him thrown out.

His funds dwindling, he intended to head to the Gulf Coast to find work in the boatyards there.

However, he wanted to be near a university to stalk fresh prey, so he went to a library and searched the college catalogues. Failing to find one on the coast, he opted for Florida State University in Tallahassee, which was just 25 miles (40 km) inland.

He left the YMCA without paying and began fruitlessly searching for a car to steal. It seemed that the drivers in Michigan, unlike those in Colorado, did not leave the keys in the ignition or tucked handily nearby. After a day trudging around in the snow, he had a despondent dinner in McDonald's and slept in a Methodist church.

Late the following afternoon, he found a Japanese car outside a repair shop. The keys were in the glove compartment. He was tired and had difficulty in finding his way out of Ann Arbor. Stopping to nap along the way, Bundy drove to Atlanta, Georgia. There, he stole a sleeping bag from a sports goods store. After meticulously wiping his finger prints from the car's interior, he dumped it with the keys in the ignition in a slum area. It was never recovered.

After watching a movie, Bundy took a Trailways bus to Tallahassee. He did not like what he found there. Although he welcomed the warmth, Florida State University, he said, looked like a large old junior college surrounded by a vast slum. He even considered moving on to the University of Florida in Gainesville, but could not afford to waste another $20 on the bus ticket.

'CHRIS M. HAGEN' MOVES INTO THE OAKS

After stashing the stolen sleeping bag and his clothes in a locker at the student bookstore, he bought a local paper and began looking for somewhere to stay. He spent the day viewing rooms. Most were more than he could afford. He now had just $160 left. A filthy upstairs room at 409 West College Avenue, a building which called itself The Oaks, was $80 a month, but the manager wanted a security deposit of $100. After finding nothing else suitable, Bundy returned there, saying he could pay $100 and would make up the difference at the end of the month. This was accepted and he rented the room under the name Chris M. Hagen. The Oaks was on the edge of campus.

The other residents remembered him as being very quiet and keeping himself to himself. They thought he was an accountant and a graduate student. He drank a lot and jogged. However, fellow resident, 19-year-old Tina Hopkins, found him odd. She later told the police: 'He just seemed real nervous. He turned his head away from us a lot. His way of talking was just real strange. It just seemed real eerie to me.'

The student employment office at Florida State University (FSU) told him that a local construction site was looking for labourers. He walked there. The foreman said he would give him a job, but he would have to produce identification. Bundy managed to steal a student ID card belonging to a Kenneth Misner, which was good enough. A stranger in town, he did not know where to get forged papers, so he applied for a duplicate birth certificate which would take some time to arrive.

When his money ran out, Bundy began stealing from supermarkets. He also stole a bicycle to get around and began breaking into cars, stealing a TV, a radio, a typewriter and a golf umbrella. These he kept, as he had no fence to sell them to.

This was a risky business. He knew each theft took him closer to being apprehended and returned to Colorado to face murder charges, but he could not help himself. He also knew that he should be off the streets by sundown, but still felt the compulsion to stay out late. Even if he did make it home by dark he would watch TV, have a few beers, then change into unobtrusive clothes and go out on the prowl. A fugitive from a jail break, he was then on the FBI's 'Ten Most Wanted' list.

Bundy had been in Tallahassee for a week when, on 14 January 1978, he stole some chicken and potato salad from the deli aisle of a supermarket. He cycled on his stolen bike to a schoolyard, where he had a solitary picnic. His knee was playing up and he wondered whether he had damaged it permanently jumping from the courthouse window during his first escape attempt. He said he could not recall what he did that evening, saying that he was 'pretty sure' he spent the night alone in his room. It was not what others would remember.

Ted Bundy was a regular at the popular disco bar Sherrod's on West Jefferson Street, just a short walk from his rooming house. It was next door to the Chi Omega sorority house and frequented by the students who lived there. One sister from 'Chi-O' named Terri Murphy, who worked there as a waitress, said that she served a lone male wearing a dark turtleneck sweater and blue jeans. He was in his early thirties – older than the normal crowd there, who tended to be in their late teens or early twenties – and he was 'overly polite'. Later, she picked him out from mugshots. It was Ted Bundy.

The man in the dark clothing was also seen by 20-year-old Connie Hastings, who arrived about 10.30 pm with Mary Ann Picano and Anna Inglett – both aged 20 – and two others. They had left their car in the parking lot behind the Chi Omega house. Sherrod's was packed, but Connie noticed the strange man watching the dance floor. It struck her that he was wearing other clothing under his dark outer garments.

'The reason I thought he was unusual was because he was scanning, scanning all the girls, just looking around. He caught my eye several times. It was a stare that kinda bothered me. I felt very uncomfortable with it,' she said.

In court, Connie picked out Bundy as the man who had stared at her.

Mary Ann Picano also saw him. He asked her if she wanted to dance. She said 'not really' and showed him that she had a drink in her hand. Bundy took it from her, saying he would put it with his own. While he was doing that Mary Ann turned to Anna Inglett and said that the man she was about to dance with 'looked like an ex-con'.

While they danced, he tried to make small talk.

'I kept concentrating on not looking at him,' she said. 'I had a really scared feeling inside. I was looking at my feet. I just looked everywhere but at him.'

After one dance Mary Ann re-joined Connie and the five women left. They had been there less than half an hour.

Carla Jean Black, a social worker who had recently graduated from FSU, arrived soon after. She also encountered a strange-looking man with an 'unnerving stare'. He fixed his gaze on her for 20 minutes and even followed her to the ladies' room. She later identified him as Ted Bundy.

A Tallahassee Police Department report on an interview they conducted with her on 18 October 1978 said: 'According to Ms. Black, at about 12.30 am on January 15 1978, she and a sorority sister of hers, Valerie Stone, went to Sherrod's. They entered into the premises and, eventually, after getting a drink she was standing around the area in the N-E portion of the building, the area that has an exit directly adjacent to the Chi-O House. Ms. Black's attention was drawn to a subject who appeared out of place, that is, he did not fit the typical college crowd. His dress and age along with his appearance, i.e. greasy-looking appearance, made him stand out to her. Moreover, this subject kept staring at her and she was afraid he was going to ask her to dance… Ms. Black states that he kept staring at her, along with many other persons, and that his mannerisms seemed to be more a "rude type of looking", "that he appeared to be smirking" or "that he felt superior" or a "I know something that you don't know attitude.'"

Tom Trice and his friend were outside, debating whether to pay the entrance fee at Sherrod's or spend the money on drink elsewhere. They saw a strange man sitting outside on a bench, even though it was freezing that night.

'He was looking kinda just spaced out,' he said. 'The guy wasn't extremely friendly.'

Soon after, a man answering the same description stepped out of the bushes nearby and followed Cheryl Rafferty as she headed home to her dormitory. When she quickened her pace, he speeded up too. Eventually she was forced to run and her stalker ran off.

The same man appears to have approached Scott Corwin and Greg Lowder after they left the disco when it closed at 2 am. They were making their way back to their Pi Kappa Alpha fraternity house when he stopped them and asked them for directions to the Holiday Inn. Lowder identified him as Bundy from a photographic line-up.

A man similarly attired had been seen earlier, peering though windows of the houses along West Pensacola Avenue.

CARNAGE AT CHI OMEGA SORORITY HOUSE

About 9.30 pm Lisa Levy, her roommate Debra O'Brian, and Melanie Nelson had left Chi Omega house and walked over to Sherrod's. Debra left with a male friend. Melanie stayed until the end, but Lisa got bored and was back in the sorority house by 11.30 pm. She watched TV in the recreation room, before going upstairs to bed at around 1.30 am.

Across the hallway, roommates Karen Chandler and Kathy Kleiner were already asleep. The room next door was occupied by Margaret Bowman and Kim Weeks, although Kim was away for the weekend. Margaret had been out with her new boyfriend Doug Johnson, who dropped her off at around 2 am. She was getting ready for bed when Melanie Nelson returned from Sherrod's with another sorority sister named Leslie Waddell and a young man. They found that the sliding glass door at the back of the house that opened into the recreation room was not closed properly. Sometimes in the cold weather the combination lock on it did not work properly.

Leslie and her friend borrowed Margaret's car to go and get a hamburger. Meanwhile, Margaret chatted with Melanie about her date. Then Nancy Dowdy returned. Her room was next to Lisa Levy and Debra O'Brian's. She found the sliding door closed properly and was in bed by 2.30 am. Terri Murphy also found the lock secure when she returned from her job at Sherrod's ten minutes later.

At 2.45 am Melanie Nelson said goodnight to Margaret Bowman and Kim Wasniewski, who had got up to go to the bathroom. Carol Johnston came home at 3 am. She found the door open and the light in the upstairs hallway switched off. While she was in the bathroom she heard the click of a doorknob. She was in bed by 3.15 am.

It was a little after 3 am when Nancy Dowdy's roommate Nita Neary got home. She too found the back door unlocked after she kissed her boyfriend goodnight. She closed and locked the door behind her and began switching off the lights in the recreation room and the living room. Then she heard a thump. Thinking her date had taken a tumble in the dark outside, she went back to the window and looked out, but he had gone.

She then heard the sound of someone running on the landing above, but assumed that she had woken one of her sorority sisters who was coming down to see her. Then she saw a man running down the stairs. He crouched at the front door and opened it with his left hand. In his right hand, he was carrying a piece of wood about two feet long.

He did not see her and she only caught a fleeting glance of him. She told the police that he was a 'white male, young, five foot eight [173 cm], 160 pounds [73 kg], thin build, clean shaven, dark complexion, large nose, dark toboggan cap, dark jacket waist-length, light-colour pants, carrying a large stick'.

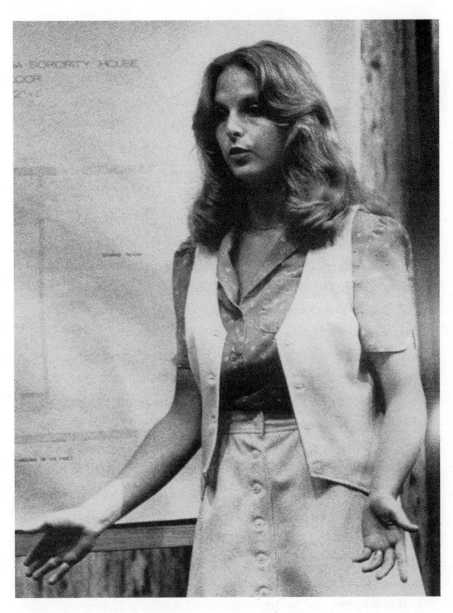

Witness Nita Neary goes over a diagram of the Chi Omega sorority house in the Ted Bundy murder trial; she said she was positive she had seen Bundy sneaking out of the house on the night when two of her sorority sisters were slain.

The description matched that of the man who had been seen lurking near Sherrod's earlier.

Nita locked the front door and went upstairs. She woke her roommate Nancy Dowdy and told her what she had seen. The two of them went back downstairs to make sure that everything was secure. Perhaps one of the sisters could have sneaked a boy into her room for a late-night tryst. But who would carry what appeared to be a club on an amorous escapade?

They decided to go back upstairs again and wake the house president Jackie McGill. Nita was explaining what had happened when Karen Chandler came staggering out of her room, bent almost double. Her face was covered in blood, although the extent of her injuries were not yet apparent. They escorted the bleeding victim to another room and a washcloth was brought to wipe her face.

Nita woke the others while Nancy called the police. Meanwhile, Jackie went into the room Karen shared with Kathy Kleiner. She found Kathy sitting cross-legged on the blood-soaked bed, rocking back and forth and moaning. Blood was pouring from her mouth. The room was splattered with blood. The attack had been so violent that there were even drops of blood on the ceiling.

Both Karen and Kathy suffered horrendous injuries. Karen's skull had been fractured, along with both her cheekbones and the orbit of her right eye. Her jaw, right arm and one finger were broken, and deep gashes and abrasions covered her face and head. Kathy also had a broken jaw and multiple cuts and contusions covered her face and head. She had also lost three teeth. The two young women were rushed to Tallahassee Memorial Hospital. After emergency surgery, they survived.

Patrolman Oscar Brannon arrived at 3.22 am. As the perpetrator had fled only minutes before he issued a BOLO – 'Be On the Look Out' – alert that was radioed to all patrol cars in the area.

There were now 40 hysterical co-eds in the hallways. Officer Henry Newkirk of the Tallahassee Police Department herded them into Carol Johnston and Helen Hayes' room. Officer Ray Crew then began searching the other rooms, accompanied by house mother Mary Crenshaw. They found Lisa Levy's room in disarray and the 20 year old lying motionless in her bed. Emergency medical technicians came running. They administered CPR – to no avail.

A quick examination of Lisa's body revealed what was first thought to be a bullet wound to the chest. But there was no exit wound. Her attacker had almost chewed her nipple off. He had also bitten her left buttock, leaving deep teeth marks. She was declared dead on arrival at Tallahassee Memorial Hospital. An autopsy discovered extensive injuries to the vagina and rectum. Later an aerosol bottle was found that had been used to sodomize her. It was covered in blood, viscera and matted hair. Lisa Levy had been severely beaten, but she died of strangulation.

The girls then noticed that 21-year-old Margaret Bowman was missing and asked Officer Newkirk to go and look for her. According to his report: 'This writer entered room #9 and immediately closed the door behind me once I observed blood on a pillow. Ms. Bowman was lying on the bed in the southwest corner of the room with her head and feet pointing in the south-north direction, respectively. The bedspread was covering Ms. Bowman's entire body with the exception of her head – which was tilted to the right lying on her pillow. (Her face was facing the west wall.) This writer pulled back the cover (bedspread) and observed Ms. Bowman had been strangled with a pair of nylon pantyhose. Her legs were bent outward slightly and spread open. (Note: Ms. Bowman was lying on her stomach.) Her right arm was extended down her side and her left arm was bent with her elbow facing east and her left hand resting on her back. Both palms of the hands were turned upwards. This writer turned Ms. Bowman over on to her right side to check for a heartbeat or pulse and discovered neither. This writer looked at Ms. Bowman's head and observed where Ms. Bowman had received a crushing blow to her right forehead coupled with what appeared to be two puncture wounds in the same vicinity. Massive bleeding occurred from both the forehead and right ear, with clotting occurring in the right ear. Additionally Ms. Bowman's neck appeared to be disjointed, leading this writer to believe there was a possible neck fracture. Ms. Bowman's body was relatively warm to the touch and her eyes were glassy with pupils dilated.... There was no evidence of a struggle either on the bed or in the room. The room was not ransacked and at this writing nothing was known to be missing.'

Patrolman Brannon, who saw the body moments later, said: 'Margaret Elizabeth Bowman was found face down on her bed... no vital signs present and no hope of gaining any.'

Unlike Lisa, Margaret had not been sexually assaulted, though her panties had been torn from her with such violence they had left burn marks. A piece of chewing gum was found in Lisa's hair. It was preserved as evidence, but as DNA testing was not available then there was nothing to tie it to Bundy. However, he had left one piece of evidence that would prove vital. It was the bite mark in Lisa's buttock. This was photographed alongside a ruler, for scale, and the flesh containing it was excised and stored.

Another piece of evidence that linked Bundy to the bludgeoned victims at the Chi Omega house was the club he had been carrying. He had taken it from the woodpile at the back of the sorority house. It was now bloody and much of the bark had been shed during the frenzied attacks. But when he left the house he was still holding on to it.

Around the time the police arrived, Yomi Segun was driving down Jefferson Street near the Chi Omega house. According to the police report: 'Mr. Segun states that he observed a white male about 5 ft 10 in [178 cm] and about 160 lbs [73 kg] wearing light brown pants, a blue coat and a dark colored knit cap walking fast westerly on Jefferson Street … This subject had brown hair and a pointed nose. He was carrying something in his left hand and holding it close to his left leg.'

Segun said that Sherrod's was closed and the man he saw walking was the only one on the streets. The police report continued: 'When asked what drew his attention to the man, Mr. Segun states that he appeared to be drunk, and it was suspicious that he was concealing the object by his left side. Mr. Segun states that he slowed down, and took a second look at the subject and got a good look at his face. Mr. Segun states that in his mind, he is positive that the subject is Theodore Bundy whose photographs he recognized in the newspapers. Mr. Segun also stated that he cannot be 100% sure, but sure enough that he is satisfied that they are one and the same.'

Four blocks west of the Chi Omega sorority house was Dunwoody Street. Around 4.15 am 20-year-old Debbie Ciccarelli in apartment 431B awoke to hear her neighbour, 21-year-old dance student Cheryl Thomas, crying and, Debbie said, 'pleading with someone'. Then she heard what she said was a 'loud pounding noise coming from the apartment'. After that, there was silence. Debbie woke her roommate Nancy Young. Both were also students at FSU. Cheryl, they thought, might be spending the night with someone, although it was unlike her. After a while they heard the sound of footsteps.

They called out to Cheryl through the thin wall. There was no response. They tried phoning her. There was no reply, but they heard someone moving around in the apartment. There was also the sound of moaning. They called the police.

When they arrived three minutes later, Officers Mitch Miller and Gerald Payne found that a window of Cheryl's apartment had been forced. Debbie had a key to the apartment to let them in. They found Cheryl lying on her bed, semi-conscious and covered in blood. She had been beaten around the head with the piece of wood that had been used to such devastating effect in Chi Omega, which now lay on the floor beside the bed. Cheryl had not been sexually assaulted, but she was naked from the waist down. Near the bed were a pair of pantyhose – Bundy's preferred ligature when strangling his victims during anal intercourse. Tests later discovered a large semen stain in Cheryl's blooded sheets. It seemed that Bundy had been interrupted before he could enjoy his ultimate pleasure and had relieved himself with masturbation while admiring his unfinished handiwork.

Cheryl Thomas survived. Like the victims at Chi Omega, she had a broken jaw. She suffered permanent loss of hearing in one ear and partial loss of balance, curtailing her career as a dancer.

Some time after 4.30 am Orley Sorrell was outside the Sigma Chi fraternity house waiting for friends he was going on a hunting expedition with. It was just one block from The Oaks.

He saw a mysterious figure dressed like the man who had been seen prowling the area earlier. Orley didn't think the man saw him, but suddenly he dashed down the street and hid in some bushes. Then he re-emerged and ran on until Orley lost sight of him near The Oaks. He was pretty sure the man was Ted Bundy.

Around that time, Henry Palumbo and Rusty Gage were returning to The Oaks where they also lived. When they arrived, they found the man they knew as Chris Hagen standing on the porch, staring blankly towards the university.

'He was in complete silence,' said Henry. 'He wasn't doing anything. He was just standing there.'

They said hello. He did not answer.

'THE SHADOW OF MURDER'

News of the attacks quickly spread and 'the shadow of murder' hung over the campus, according to the *Tallahassee Democrat*.

The whole city was terrified. Sales of guns and ammunition soared and locksmiths found themselves in demand. A team of FSU officials visited the sorority houses, telling the residents: 'We're here because we want to tell you the facts, and we want to put the fear of the Lord in you. We have a deranged murderer on our hands. We don't know where he is, why he is doing it, what he will do next.' Female students were told not to walk anywhere alone, day or night.

The murders were also a topic of conversation among the residents of The Oaks. Henry Palumbo was speculating that the killer had stayed in town after the attacks, when Bundy jumped in.

'He thought it was somebody very professional and that he had done it before,' Palumbo said. 'He also said it was kind of smart how the guy used a weapon that couldn't be traced. It sorta struck me as funny because I hadn't heard that over the radio or anything.'

Rusty Gage also had a discussion about the murders with the man they knew as Chris Hagen. According to Gage, Hagen had loftily derided the police. 'I know myself that I could get away with any crime I wanted to – even murder if I really wanted to – because I know how to get around the law,' Hagen had said.

Gage had not taken this too seriously, as Chris Hagen, he said, 'was just one of those people who casts weird vibes at you. He usually wanted to tell us how great he was. He wanted people to acknowledge that he was a great person. Apparently, no one ever had.'

By coincidence, the forensic anthropologist who had examined the remains of Janice Ott and Denise Naslund on the hillside near Issaquah, Washington State, was in Tallahassee visiting a former student who was then teaching at Florida State University. The Chi Omega murders reminded them of the 'Ted' killings three years before. When the *Seattle Times* ran an Associated Press report on the attacks, the similarities were not lost on local journalists either.

Bob Keppel phoned the Tallahassee Police Department and gave them a description of Bundy, along with his back story. Criminal investigator Michael Fisher was on an FBI course at Quantico, Virginia. Deputy District Attorney Milton Blakey, who was handling the case in Colorado, called him, then sent a package on Bundy and his modus operandi to Tallahassee.

CHAPTER EIGHT
Lake City

TED BUNDY had just one month of freedom left. With Tallahassee on lockdown, he was unlikely to find any new prey there. But he had already made provision. Three days before the murders Bundy had taken the keys from a white Dodge van parked outside Florida State University's media centre. He had them copied and returned them a few days later. The matter had been reported to the campus police, but after the attacks at the Chi Omega house they had more important matters to worry about and there was no reason to think that the disappearance of the keys and their mysterious return had anything to do with the murders.

Also on 12 January, Bundy stole the Florida licence plate 13-D-1130 from a Volkswagen camper van belonging to Randy Regan parked behind Cheryl Thomas' Dunwoody Street apartment. Again there was no reason to make any connection.

After the murders, Bundy continued to support himself by shoplifting and the theft of cash and credit cards. On 21 January he visited a supermarket in Tallahassee's Northward Mall and stole the purse of Mrs Mark Labadie from her grocery trolley. He took $20 in cash from it and left the pocket book in a dumpster, only to retrieve it later as it contained her husband's credit cards. Bundy should have been more circumspect when it came to using credit cards; after all, his use of a Chevron gas card had given Colorado criminal investigator Michael Fisher his first break in the Caryn Campbell case. Even so, that night Bundy used Mark Labadie's Visa to pay for his dinner in a restaurant.

The following Saturday he used stolen credit cards to buy over $150-worth of tennis gear and clothing in five stores. Four days later he bought more shirts and socks using Mark Labadie's credit card again. Then on Friday he lifted Kathy Evans' father's credit cards from her purse in the university's library. He went on a $260 spending spree that afternoon, buying a pipe, tobacco and a lighter, as well as bed linen, towels, shoes, a belt, luggage and clothes – including more socks. Bundy later admitted to having a foot fetish.

That evening he took a risk by returning to Sherrod's where he stole four purses and handbags. He stole another young woman's purse at Big Daddy's Lounge the following night.

The next day, Sunday 5 February, Bundy used the duplicate car keys to steal the white van from outside the university's media centre. Then he changed the plates with those he had stolen.

The following morning, he went on yet another shopping spree using stolen cards.

Had he headed northwards out of the state he might have got away with the murder and mayhem he had caused in Florida. Tallahassee is less than 20 miles (32 km) from the Georgia state line. Instead he travelled eastwards along Interstate-10 towards Jacksonville, which is 160 miles (257 km) away. A white van carrying the Florida licence plate number 13-D-11300 stopped for petrol just north of Lake City before noon on 7 February. According to gas station attendant Martha Jean Stephens, it was driven by a nervous young man in a grey tracksuit who had 'scary blue eyes'. He paid with a Gulf credit card belonging to William R. Evans, Kathy's dad.

The same licence plate was recorded again at a gas station in Jacksonville three hours later. The attendant remembers that the name on the credit card did not match the 'celebrity name tag' on his coat. Later that night, William Evans' Mastercard was used to buy dinner at the Holiday Inn in Orange Park, 10 miles (16 km) south of Jacksonville. Other customers thought he was 'weird-looking' and probably drunk. 'William Evans' then checked into the Holiday Inn in Jacksonville, leaving the following morning without checking out at the front desk.

A man later identified as Ted Bundy bought a hunting knife with a ten-inch blade from Green Acres Sporting Goods store in Jacksonville. Mark Labadie's Gulf card was used to buy petrol and a road map early in the morning of Wednesday 8 February.

AN ABDUCTION THWARTED, YET ANOTHER HORRIFIC ATTACK

Next, Bundy parked the van in the parking lot of the K-Mart shopping centre across the road from the Jed Stuart Junior High School. Fourteen-year-old Leslie Ann Parmenter had crossed the road to meet her brother Danny, who was coming to pick her up. Instead, a white van stopped in front of her and a man got out, leaving the driver's door open. He came to talk to her. She said: 'He was dark-haired, messy-haired, sloppily dressed. He had a couple days' growth of beard and a moustache. He had on an over jacket and he had on a badge that said, "Fire Department, Richard Burton". It was plastic, like a plastic badge with a white tag inside of it.'

She also noticed that he was nervous and fidgety, 'digging in his pockets like he didn't know what he was going to say next'. He asked her if she went to school over the road and was heading for K-Mart. Before she could answer, her brother Danny pulled up in his truck.

'I stuck my head out of the window and asked my sister what he wanted,' said Danny Parmenter. 'She said she didn't know and I told her to walk around to my side of the truck. I asked the man: "What do you want?" and he started going back to the van. So I got out of the truck and I went up to the man and asked him again what he wanted. He was acting very nervous and he started rolling up his window while I was still askin' him what he wanted. He said: "I just asked her a question and she told me she couldn't answer it," or something like that. And he rolled up his window in the van and started to drive off.'

Danny Parmenter quickly noted down the van's licence plate number. He also noted that the van was dirty, as if it had been driven out in the boondocks. Then he tried to follow it, but lost the van in heavy traffic. He then drove home and gave the licence number to his father, who was a policeman.

That night, a man answering Bundy's new dishevelled description checked into the Holiday Inn in Lake City using a Visa card bearing the name of Ralf Miller. His speech was slurred and he appeared drunk.

A maid said he had 'funny eyes', but no one questioned him when his bought dinner using a credit card in one name and drinks using a second credit card bearing another. He left in the morning without checking out.

Bundy headed east along US Route 90. Where it becomes Duval Street, he spotted Lake City Junior High School, where 12-year-old Kimberly Diane Leach was in the seventh grade. Her first class was gym, but she had to return to the main building to retrieve her purse. The last time she was seen, she was returning to the gym.

There were a number of reports of a white van circling the school that afternoon. A firefighter named C.L. 'Andy' Andersen was approaching the school on the way back from a nightshift when he saw a 'scowling' man answering Bundy's description leaving the school, holding a young girl by the arm. She was crying. The man shoved her into the passenger side of a white van, then jogged around to the driver's door. Anderson recalled thinking: 'Daddy's going to take that little girl home and give her a spanking.'

In the van, it was thought that Kimberly put up a fight. The van was seen weaving as it travelled down US Route 90. A woman coming the other way said that the van nearly ran her off the road. He may have knocked the child out as he drove on for 28 miles (45 km), exiting at Live Oak. Her body was found in an empty hog shed 13 miles (21 km) further down the road. It appeared that he had forced her to lie on her stomach and then, while he was raping her from behind, he stabbed her and cut her throat.

That afternoon Kimberly's mother reported her missing and a search began. By that time Bundy was back in Tallahassee. He dumped the van within the city limits and wiped down any areas where he may have left fingerprints. He also removed the stolen licence plate but did not destroy it or throw it away. Another mistake.

When he returned to The Oaks, Kenneth Misner's duplicate birth certificate had arrived in the post. With a false identity, Bundy could now get work and had no reason not to move on. Indeed, he was a week behind with the rent. He dined out on William Evans' Mastercard. The following day he stole a green Toyota, ready to make his escape from Florida. He planned to head for Houston, Texas, leaving no later than 11 pm that night. Instead, he took a young woman from The Oaks named Frances Messier to a stylish French restaurant named Chez Pierre. Then they went back to his room to watch *The Rockford Files* on a stolen TV. It was not until after 1 am that he started loading the stolen goods he had accumulated into the Toyota.

Already on the alert, this attracted the attention of the cops. Leon County Deputy Sheriff Keith Dawes pulled up behind the Toyota and asked Bundy for identification. He had none on him.

'Where do you live?' asked Deputy Dawes.

'College Avenue,' said Bundy.

The driver's lack of ID made Deputy Dawes suspicious, so he began examining the car. The deputy shone his flashlight through the car's window and spotted the stolen licence plate, which Bundy had hung on to, on the floor.

Deputy Dawes walked back to his patrol car to call in the licence plate number 13-D-11300 and have it checked out. Bundy seized the opportunity to make a run for it. He dashed across the road, around the back of an apartment block, then jumped over the fence into the backyard of The Oaks and hid in some bushes. Realizing that pursuit was futile, Deputy Dawes stayed behind to impound the car and its contents.

Bundy waited in the bushes, listening for the sound of a pursuer. When he heard none, he scurried across the yard and up the fire escape to his room. He spent the rest of the night there in the dark.

The following morning he inexplicably changed into tennis gear and went to the office of the building manager Robert Fulford, telling him that he was expecting to receive some money from his mother in Michigan which would cover the rent arrears, even faking a long distance call to Ann Arbor – although Fulford remembered it as Wisconsin. During this pantomime, Bundy noticed the calling card of a police detective on the manager's desk. The cops were closing in. Nevertheless, he spent the rest of the day playing racquetball and riding his bike, even though he could not be sure that the police would not be waiting for him when he returned to his room.

He remained at large and the next day, Sunday 12 February, he went out in search of another car to steal. At around 11 am he found a 1972 Mazda in the parking lot of a Mormon church on Stadium Drive. The keys were in the ignition. He got in and drove off, but the car was in such bad shape that he abandoned it and looked for something better.

'I DIDN'T WANT TO TAKE ANYBODY'S CAR'

Across the street, he spotted a 1968 Volkswagen Beetle, like the one he used to own. As soon as it started up, he realized that the engine had been souped up. There were other personal touches and, while raping, killing and maiming young women and children affected him not at all, he felt guilty about stealing this car.

Later he told detectives: 'I looked at it and it was obvious, some, somebody's little pride and joy had souped it up and I know I wasn't looking... I didn't want to take anybody's car like, you know, I felt that couldn't afford, you know, I don't know to say these things but it kind of sounds odd maybe to you but here, this was obviously, this was a girl's car first of all because it has these little trinkets hanging down and the books and things, kinds of things in a car that a girl would have in the car, and I said, Jesus, man, don't take her car, you know. I felt, you know, I didn't want to take it, believe it or not, I mean I'm telling you straight, I just said, what are [we] going to do. I had the damn thing and I said why don't we use it to look for another car so I just used it to look for another car.'

It was just after 11 pm when he spotted another VW Beetle. The orange 1972 Beetle belonged to Ricky Garzaniti, who had parked it outside 515 East Georgia Street while he and his wife popped inside to collect their child. Thinking they would only be gone a moment, he had left the keys in the ignition. But they got talking and when the Garzanitis emerged at 11.15 pm the car was gone.

Bundy drove back to The Oaks to collect the rest of his things and wipe the room – including the ceiling – of fingerprints. Then he took the Interstate-10 road westwards towards Pensacola and the Alabama state line, well over 200 miles (322 km) away.

But Bundy's luck was running out fast. He discovered that when he approached 50 miles (80 km) an hour one of the rear wheels began to vibrate, shaking the whole car and forcing him to slow down. Construction work on the interstate highway forced traffic on to the two-lane Highway 90. Driving slowly caused a tailback that risked drawing the attention of the police, but this was relieved when he pulled into rest stops for fitful naps.

After nursing the crippled VW Beetle for 154 miles (248 km), he pulled into a garage in Crestville, Florida, just 35 miles (56 km) from Pensacola and still 120 miles (193 km) from the state line. He asked to have the tyre changed, but the mechanic said there were none of the right size in the shop.

Bundy went to the Holiday Inn for breakfast, but when he tried to pay with a credit card the waitress discovered it had been reported stolen. He was forced to flee, with the waitress and her gun-toting manager in hot pursuit.

Revving up the car and making a clean getaway, Bundy decided that he should hide during daylight hours. Several miles on he turned down a dirt road and pulled up on a slope. What he did not know was that he had parked on a restricted area of Elgin Air Force Base.

As well as the roar of jet engines he could hear the flutter of helicopter rotor blades. Unsure whether the choppers were hunting him, he slept fitfully during the day. When it grew dark, he tried to back the car back up the slope, but the earth was too soft. He tried putting everything he could find under the back wheels – including the back seat – but still the tyres would not grip. After three hours or so, he gave up. Taking his backpack, he tried hitchhiking back to the interstate highway.

He got a lift with an airman in civilian clothes who was interested in why Bundy was out there on his own. Nevertheless, he dropped Bundy off at a gas station where he persuaded an attendant to drive him back to the car and help him push it back up to the road. The obliging attendant told Bundy that he was lucky the military police had not arrested him. It happened to his friends all the time.

When Bundy reached Pensacola he tried to check into a motel using another credit card. But it was blocked because it too had been reported stolen. Bundy feigned surprise, saying that it had gone missing but had been found again and he said he would go and get cash. Another restaurant chased him out and he was forced to sleep in the car.

In the morning he had breakfast and shaved and showered in the locker room of a community college near Pensacola Airport, where he also changed his clothes. Then he went to the launderette and spent the rest of the day on the beach.

That evening he had an early dinner. It was St Valentine's Day and couples were out celebrating. Bundy drank a lot. Then he went to a shopping mall to buy more clothes, particularly socks. Short of cash, he went to a bar with the aim of stealing more wallets and purses, but a waitress saw him rifling through a woman's handbag and called the bouncers.

They questioned him in a backroom, but the young woman whose handbag he had been dipping into said nothing was missing. Nevertheless, he was asked to leave. It was around 1.30 am on the morning of Wednesday 15 February.

APPREHENDED EN ROUTE TO ALABAMA

Although he was drunk Bundy decided to head on to Alabama and comparative safety. However, he missed his turning on the freeway and got lost in an industrial area of the city. He was driving in the Pensacola suburb of Brownsville with his lights off when he was spotted by Patrolman David Lee, who called in the licence plate number and quickly discovered that the car was stolen. When Bundy saw the patrol car in his rear view mirror, there was little he could do. He could hardly attempt to outrun the cop in a crippled VW Beetle, so he pulled quietly over to the side of the road.

Patrolman Lee drew his revolver as he got out of the car and ordered the driver to lay face down on the road. He had got one handcuff closed around the suspect's wrist when Bundy rolled over and struck him in the face.

Then he kicked the arresting officer's feet out from under him. Patrolman Lee fired, but missed. Bundy ran for it, with the officer close behind.

Bundy could have escaped, but kept turning to see if the cop was closing in. Patrolman Lee saw a glint. Possibly it came from the handcuffs that were still attached to the suspect's wrist, but maybe he had a gun. He fired again. Bundy fell, although he had not been hit.

Patrolman Lee approached what he imagined to be a dead or injured man lying on the ground. As he leaned over the incapacitated figure, Bundy kicked his feet from under him once more and called out for help. A local resident came out of his house, but seeing that the altercation involved a police officer, quickly retreated inside.

Instead of firing again Patrolman Lee clubbed his adversary around the head with the barrel of his revolver. Bleeding, Bundy fell to the ground. Back-up units of the Pensacola Police Department were soon on the scene. Patrolman Lee secured the handcuffs around the captive's other wrist and led his prisoner back to his car.

On the way to the police station Bundy said to Patrolman Lee: 'I wish you had just killed me back there.' The officer said that he did not want to kill him. After all, so far the suspect was only facing charges of being in possession of a stolen car and resisting arrest. But Bundy was insistent. 'If I run at the jail, will you shoot me?'

Bundy gave his name as Kenneth Raymond Misner and his address as 982 West Brevard Street, Tallahassee, Florida. He was found to be in possession of 21 stolen credit cards, some of which had been gleaned from burglaries in the Tallahassee area. By and large the credit cards and IDs in his possession belonged to co-eds at Florida State University. Detective Norman Chapman of Pensacola PD called the Tallahassee PD, who sent Detective Don Patchen and Leon County Investigator Steven Bodiford. The following day they began questioning the John Doe that Pensacola PD had in custody. They already knew that the suspect was not Kenneth Misner, as the real Kenneth Misner, a well-known former FSU track star, had already been contacted by the police.

Bundy admitted stealing the orange VW Beetle and was arraigned on charges of grand larceny and the possession of stolen property. Isaac Koran, an attorney from the local public defender's office, quickly realized that there was more to this case when the State Attorney Curtis Golden appeared at the arraignment. Koran also discovered that his client had made a call to Atlanta, where he tried to contact Millard Farmer, a famous defence attorney in potential death penalty cases who Bundy had been in touch with over the Caryn Campbell charges in Colorado. Farmer was a director of Team Defense Project Inc., and a militant opponent of capital punishment. Koran called Farmer and discovered that the name of his client was Ted Bundy. With detectives arriving from Tallahassee, it became clear to Koran that they were interested in the Chi Omega case.

Koran called Michael Minerva, the Tallahassee public defender. They agreed that Bundy should not talk to the police.

However, their client was determined to cut his own deal. He agreed to tell the detectives his real name, provided he was allowed to use the telephone and they delayed making the announcement of his recapture.

He called Liz Kendall. She was later questioned by Washington State detective Bob Keppel about that call. When Bundy told her that he was in custody in Florida, she asked him whether it had something to do with the murder of the sorority girls. He said he did not want to talk about it. He did not want to talk about the murders in Washington State either. He said he was sick.

'I asked him if somehow I had played a part in what had happened,' Liz told Keppel. 'He said no. For years before he even met me he'd been fighting the same sickness and that when it broke we just happened to be together.'

She had then asked Bundy if he had ever tried to kill her. He said that one time he did.

'He told me that he was really trying to control this sickness and that he'd been staying off the streets and trying to be normal,' she told Keppel, 'and that it just happened that I was there when he felt it coming on and that he wanted to kill me that night.'

The night in question was in the autumn of 1973, she thought. He had tried stopping her chimney up and placed towels around the bottom of the door. She awoke gasping for air and threw a window open.

They talked about a phone call he had made to her from Salt Lake City late at night when a young woman – presumably Debra Kent – had been abducted.

'I always thought well, he couldn't be out abducting women because I'd talked to him on the phone that night,' she said, 'and I asked if he didn't sometimes call me or come over to touch base with reality after he'd done some of these things, and he said, "That's a pretty good guess."'

Again she asked him specifically about the murders in Florida, but he said he did not want to talk about it.

They spoke again two days later.

'Then the next Saturday morning at two he called again, collect, and he said he wanted to talk about what we'd been talking about in the first phone call. And I said: "You mean about being sick?" And he said: "Yes …". He told me that he was sick and was consumed by something he didn't understand, and … that he just couldn't contain it.'

Keppel asked Liz why Bundy couldn't control himself.

'Well, he said that he tried, he said that it took so much of his time, and that's why he wasn't doing well in law school; and that he couldn't seem to get his act together, because he spent so much time trying to maintain a normal life and he just couldn't do it. He said that he was preoccupied with this force … He mentioned an incident about following a sorority girl … he didn't do anything that night, but … he just told me that's how it was, that he was out late at night and he would follow people like that, but that he'd try not to but he just did it anyway….'

The Washington State murders came up in conversation.

'He did talk about Lake Sammamish, he told me that he was, he started by saying that he was sick, and he said: "I don't have a split personality, and I don't have black-outs." He said:

"I remember everything that I've done." And he mentioned the day, July 14, when two women were abducted from Lake Sammamish and we went out to eat around 5 pm and he was saying that he remembered that he ate two hamburgers and enjoyed every bite of it. And that we went to Ferrell's and he said that it wasn't that he had forgotten what he'd done that day or that he couldn't remember, but just said that it was over.'

Liz went on to press him on the murders in Tallahassee.

'I asked him specifically about the Florida murders,' she said. 'And he told me he didn't want to talk about them, but then in the phone conversation he said that he felt like he had a disease like alcoholism or something like alcoholics that couldn't take another drink, and he told me it was just something that he couldn't be around and he knew it now. And I asked him what that was and he said: 'Don't make me say it.'"

PLAYING GAMES WITH INTERROGATORS

The identity of the man in custody was confirmed as Ted Bundy when his fingerprints matched those supplied by the FBI. Even though he had been advised not to talk to the police, Bundy continued his meetings with Florida detectives Chapman, Patchen and Bodiford, giving them the impression that he was on the verge of giving them a full confession. But he asked for the tape recorder to be turned off when he discussed his taste for voyeurism and pornography, and what he referred to as 'my problem'. Asked directly if he had killed the young women in the Chi Omega sorority house in Tallahassee, he said: 'The evidence is there. Look for it.'

Detective Patchen pressed him on this.

'I asked him whether or not, directly, if he had killed the girls at the Chi Omega house in Tallahassee,' he said, 'and he had stated that if he was pressured into giving an answer that that answer would be no. And in that context of saying that, he would tell us that he didn't want to lie to us. But again if he was pressured into answering, he would have to say, no. Of course he explained to us the facts that he had built up in his mind never [to] reveal certain information, that he wanted to tell us but he couldn't.'

Detective Chapman tried another approach, telling Bundy about his two daughters and how he felt about them in an attempt to soften him up.

'So I want to help all the little girls in the world,' he said to Bundy. 'And I want you, I want you to tell me right now, I want you to start, start with Chi Omega. Tell me how it felt when you walked in there … when you knew you were going to kill. Come on, Ted, open up. Talk. You talked to us before, tell me how it felt when you went in there. Tell me what it was that caused you to go in there.'

'I can't, I can't talk about it,' said Bundy.

'You'd be a fool, yeah, you'd be a fool,' Detective Chapman continued.

'I can't talk about it,' Bundy insisted.

'You'd be a fool that was helping more people than he could ever imagine. So tell me about it.'

'I can't talk about this situation.'

The other interrogators fared no better. After interviewing Bundy, Investigator Bodiford said: 'We'd talk about what we'd refer to as a problem. You know, "You have a problem. You do this and this." Generally, it was my impression and the impression of the other investigators, and I feel that it was Ted's impression, that when I said problem, I meant killing people. But did I come right out and say: "Look, did you commit those murders in Washington that they say you committed?" No, I never asked him like that.'

'I want you to understand me so you can understand my problem,' Bundy said, adding that he never enjoyed the act, but had to do it to keep his fantasies alive. 'The act was a downer. What was the act – I'm not going to tell you the modus operandi.'

He also said: 'Sometimes I feel like a vampire,' insisting, 'I never hurt anyone I knew.'

Talking of a young woman he had seen when out cycling, he said: 'I had to have her at any cost.' Nothing more.

The police then discovered Bundy's link to the disappearance of Kimberly Leach through the white Dodge van stolen by Bundy from Florida State University's media centre, which had been found abandoned in Tallahassee on 13 February. Lester Parmenter in Jacksonville had reported that his daughter Leslie had been approached by a man diving a white Dodge van carrying the licence plate number 13-D-11300.

This had been recovered later from the stolen green Toyota after Bundy had fled. The use of one of the stolen credit cards Bundy was carrying put him in Jacksonville on the day of Danny Parmenter's encounter with the white van driver, and in Lake City the following day, when Kimberley Leach disappeared. Investigator Bodiford sent mug shots of Bundy back to the Tallahassee Police Department, where Deputy Dawes confirmed that he was indeed the man with the green Toyota and the 13-D-11300 licence plates.

Bundy liked playing games, coming tantalizingly near to making a confession.

'We talked one night about his car, for example. He said the front seat was either loose or out of it, the right front of his Volkswagen,' said Investigator Bodiford.

'Why?' Investigator Bodiford had asked.

'Well, I can carry things easier that way,' Bundy replied.

'You mean you can carry bodies easier that way?'

'Well, let's just say I can carry cargo better that way,' said Bundy.

So Investigator Bodiford asked: 'That cargo you carried, was it sometimes... was it damaged?'

'Sometimes it was damaged and sometimes it wasn't,' said Bundy.

Bundy was afraid because Florida had reinstituted the use of the electric chair in 1976 and, in an attempt to coax a confession out of him, the detectives showed him Florida's Mentally Disordered Sex Offender statute, under which he would be given treatment rather than being executed. Bundy dismissed this, saying it did not apply to him as he was neither guilty nor mentally ill.

They also tried to get him to talk about Kimberley Leach, who they were certain he had murdered. Bundy merely said that her fate was 'horrible', telling them that they 'wouldn't want to see her.'

Kimberly Leach was only 12 years old when she disappeared.

Later, when Bundy was acting as his own attorney, he deposed Detective Chapman on his questions about Kimberly Leach.

'I said: "Ted, I will go," to the best of my knowledge, "and locate the girl, find the body and let her parents know where she's at,"' Detective Chapman had said. 'And Mr Bundy replied that "I cannot do that to you because the sight is too horrible to look at."'

Again, they begged Bundy to tell them where Kimberly's body could be found, but he remained unmoved by any appeal to human sentiment.

'He was sitting kind of slumped in a chair, you know, kind of sitting next to a desk with his arm on it, kind of leaning over,' said Investigator Bodiford. 'There was a pack of cigarettes on the desk, an empty pack.... We were talking to him and trying to really impress him that he should, you know, ease these people's minds.... He raised up in the chair and grabbed the pack of cigarettes and crumpled them and threw them on the floor and said: "But I'm the most cold-hearted son of a bitch you'll ever meet."'

Detective Chapman also knew of Bundy's conversations with Liz Kendall and pressed him on them.

'Ted I think that you have talked to Liz the way you're talking to us now, I think Liz probably told you or you have agreed, or reached an agreement that you need to get it all cleared up,' said Detective Chapman.

'That's correct,' said Bundy

'She understands and the fact that she realizes the magnitude of what we're talking about. And she realizes, maybe not all of it, but she realizes that you're involved in it,' Detective Chapman continued.

'And she knows no details,' said Bundy.

'So she's not gonna be hurt anymore,' said Detective Chapman.

Bundy grunted in response.

'Certainly she is. I'm sure you believe that she knows,' Detective Chapman went on.

'Right,' said Bundy.

Bundy said he would talk to Liz again that night.

'I've got a lot of friends that stick with me through thick and thin,' he said. They seemed almost immune to the horror. One of them was Carole Boone, who he called and wrote to almost every day.

She had been contacted repeatedly by the FBI when he was at large and was bothered by the Chi Omega sorority house connection. He must tell her the truth, no matter how horrible, she had said.

Instead, on 28 February 1978, in a letter to her, he dismissed the FBI as 'Fornicators, Bastards and Imposters'. He went on to evoke her sympathy by describing the dark cell he was kept in and the cockroaches that shared his food, concluding the letter with: 'I love you Boone. I need you. More than ever.'

Later letters addressed her as 'Darling Boone', 'Tender Peach-blossom', 'Precious Fleshpot' and 'My Beloved Quintessential Quark'. In her replies she called him 'Dearest Bunzo', 'Darling Bunnykins', 'Sweet Theodore' and 'Angelbuns', and she dropped all doubts about his innocence.

Bundy also told the detectives he had a plan. It was clear that this was to continue bargaining with them, intimating that he might be persuaded to make a full confession if he could be transferred to a prison in Washington State where he could be nearer to his family.

'I'm interested in clearing everything up,' said Bundy. 'It requires talking to… starting with somebody in Seattle, and to make some inquiries, and it requires talking to somebody in Utah, to make some inquiries.'

He said he wanted 'everybody being satisfied… to get all the answers they want to all the questions they want to all the questions they want to ask, then after that was all over, I would like to go back to Washington State. That's where my mother is, that's where my family is, and that's where I'm from…. Washington has a lot of questions to ask me.'

Detective Chapman explained that even if they did extradite him back to Washington State to stand trial, he would then have to be returned to Florida to face charges there.

'I'm not talking about trials,' said Bundy. 'There would be no need for trials. Ted Bundy wants something out of this and maybe that's not right and maybe he doesn't deserve it…. Ted Bundy wants to survive, too…. I have responsibilities to my parents…. That's part of it and the second part is getting out of the limelight as quickly as possible, without all these horrendous trials.'

As well as being back close to his parents, Bundy expressed a wish of 'giving knowledge and peace of mind that can be returned to people who don't know what happened….'

And '…to their loved ones,' Detective Chapman added.

Detectives Chapman and Patchen and Investigator Bodiford continued to listen to Bundy's offer of admitting murder, before telling him that extradition to Washington State was not going to happen – at least until the murders in Florida were dealt with. Detective Patchen then asked how many states he could be wanted in. Bundy said six. The detectives also made it absolutely clear that they were convinced that he was responsible for the murder of the Chi Omega students and the abduction and murder of Kimberly Leach. The people of Washington State would have to be content with whatever justice Florida meted out, they said. Nor would he be returned to Colorado, where he had escaped twice, nor Utah, where he faced only a relatively short sentence for aggravated kidnapping.

It was then discovered that cigarette butts found in the stolen white Dodge van matched those in a pile found in a wooded area some 30 miles (48 km) west of Lake City in the way they had been smoked and stubbed out. Accessible by a dirt road near the entrance of Suwannee River State Park, it was the perfect spot for a murder. A local meatpacker dumped waste there, which attracted scavengers and littered the area with bones.

The Chief Medical Examiner Peter Lipkovic, said: 'After initial photography of the intact hog shed and the parts of the body that were visible from the outside, the roof of the hog shed and the wall that it was leaning onto were removed and further photography and examination of the body were performed. The body was resting on its left side with the left thigh and knee drawn up close and the right leg resting on the left thigh with the hip and knee joints at approximately right angles. The left arm was stretched out straight and resting underneath the left thigh parallel to the long axis of the torso and protruding underneath both thighs being parallel to the right lower leg. The abdomen and chest were resting as follows: the abdomen partially resting on its left and left posterior aspects, and the chest and upper shoulder area being flat on the back. The right arm was stretched straight up with a slight bend in the elbow joint going past and slightly encircling the head. The head was resting on its right side facing the upper right arm and being immediately adjacent to it. The only clothing item on the body was a stained, off-white appearing body shirt with a short turtleneck and long sleeves… The body was subsequently transported to the Medical Examiner's Office and further examination revealed that the entire intact area of the body skin surfaces was mummified (parchment-like skin). The skin of the right side of the face and scalp… was absent and completely skeletonized. The remaining scalp, including the left ear and the skin of the left face, was mummified and intact showing intact orbital openings, nostrils, and an oral opening. The skin of the entire neck area, anterior and posterior, was absent. This skin loss extended into the upper chest area to approximately the level of the sternoclavicular joint. The edges of this skin defect were rounded and weathered, hence no determination of the exact nature of this injury can be made.… There was a large area of missing skin and internal organs starting at the pubic mound 3 inches below the navel and proceeding through the inguinal regions, bilaterally, the inner thighs, and up to the level of the coccyx.'

Dr Lipkovic saw evidence of sexual battery in the vaginal and anal regions of a 'type undetermined' and concluded that 'Kimberly Diane Leach died of homicidal violence to the neck region, type undetermined.'

Kimberly Leach had been missing for 57 days when her body was found. Decomposition would have accounted for some of the loss of flesh, along with animal predation. The positioning of the body led Dr Lipkovic to speculate that the girl had been on all fours when her throat was slit from behind.

This report would be fiercely disputed in court. However, now that the body of Kimberly Leach had been discovered, the authorities in Florida would find it relatively easy to convict Bundy of her murder.

CHAPTER NINE

Insane?

AT 3PM ON 27 JULY 1978 the indictments for the Chi Omega sorority house attacks were handed down by the Grand Jury in Tallahassee, Florida. The indictment for the kidnap and murder of 12-year-old Kimberly Leach would soon follow. However, any trial concerning Kimberly in Suwannee County would have to wait until proceedings over the Chi Omega murders in Leon County were completed. Although both incidents took place in the state of Florida, they were not clearly related, so they would have to be tried separately by local prosecutors. In all, some 60 felony warrants had be filed in Tallahassee and Pensacola following Bundy's recapture. Colorado wanted him for the murder of Caryn Campbell and two jail breaks. Utah wanted him back to complete his sentence for kidnapping Carol DaRonch, and charges in Washington State and Idaho were likely to follow.

Ted Bundy, legal files in hand and enigmatic smile on his features, is escorted from Leon County courthouse after a circuit judge refused to order him to furnish the prosecution with hair, blood, saliva or handwriting specimens.

Despite his protests, Bundy loved the limelight. He was furious when the court prevented him giving face-to-face interviews from jail, ruling that any pre-trial publicity might damage his own interests. Nevertheless, he found himself involuntarily attending a press conference. This was held for the benefit of his jailer Sheriff Ken Katsaris, who faced re-election. Sheriff Katsaris called it for 9.30 pm that evening. When reporters and TV crews arrived, he was turned out in his best black suit with a white shirt and striped tie.

Bundy was in Pensacola that day and had been back in his cell for an hour when he was dragged out of solitary confinement to be paraded in front of the television cameras. He was wearing prison slippers and a baggy green jumpsuit. This contrasted with his face, which had a deathly white jail pallor. As he emerged from the lift, the TV cameras dazzled him. Unprepared, he retreated back into the lift. Soon realizing that there was no place to hide, he re-emerged, while Katsaris opened the sealed indictment and began reading: 'In the name of, and by the authority of the state of Florida…'

Bundy interrupted.

'What do we have here, Ken?' he said. 'Let's see. Oh, an indictment! Why don't you read it to me? You're running for re-election.'

There was little love lost between Bundy and Sheriff Katsaris, who tried to deny him all the privileges he had enjoyed elsewhere. In front of the media Bundy pointedly turned his back on Sheriff Katsaris and leaned against the wall, all the cameras turned on him as the sheriff continued reading: '…the said Theodore Robert Bundy did make an assault upon Karen Chandler and/or Kathy Kleiner…'

Bundy seized the opportunity to address the reporters.

'He said he was going to get me,' Bundy said. Then he directed his remarks to the sheriff.

'Okay. You got your indictment,' he said. 'That's all you're going to get.'

Sheriff Katsaris ignored him and continued reading: '…did then and there unlawfully kill a human being, to wit: Lisa Levy, by strangling and/or beating her until she was dead, and said killing was perpetrated by said Theodore Robert Bundy, and did then and there unlawfully kill a human being, to wit: Margaret Bowman, by strangling and/or beating her until she was dead… and that Theodore Robert Bundy, from or with a premeditated design or intent to effect the death of said Cheryl Thomas…'

Bundy did what he could to make a mockery of the reading, raising his hand at one point and saying: 'I'll plead not guilty right now.'

Sheriff Katsaris continued reading while Bundy asked: 'Can I speak to the press when you're done?'

The disruption continued.

'We've displayed the prisoner now,' Bundy said mockingly. 'I think it's my turn. Listen, I've been kept in isolation for six months. You've been talking for six months. I'm gagged… you're not gagged.'

When the reading of the indictment was completed, Bundy was served his copy. On the way back to the elevator he turned to the cameras, held up the papers and tore them in half.

Showing such public contempt for the law may have prejudiced the case, but Bundy was determined to vent his anger at the system which, he said, convicted him in the media before he was allowed to face his accusers and their 'meagre' evidence in court. He wrote to *The New York Times* bureau chief in Miami, Jon Nordheimer, saying: 'I am sick and tired of publicity, no matter how neat the format or prestigious the publication. The articles about me... all tend to read remarkably alike. I can only marvel at the singular lack of originality among journalists.

Ted Bundy waves to TV cameras as his indictment for the murder of FSU co-eds is read out at the Leon County Jail. Bundy wanted to make a statement to the press but was not allowed to do so.

The did-he-or-didn't-he articles have become tiresome, since there is invariably left the lingering inference: How-could-he-not-have? With the relentlessness of a starfish set upon prying open a clam, *The Times* moves toward the publication of a story, and all this clam wants is a word or two before dinner time. I have never had the opportunity to address myself fully to all the accusations, inferences, innuendo, rumors and suspicion *ad nauseum*. What has irked me about the stories written on my case is that anyone with a badge or a bachelor of arts degree is considered an expert on Theodore Bundy and what makes him tick. Prosecutors, policemen, journalists, old girlfriends, friends and family of the "victims", psychologists, psychiatrists, ex-roommates, former teachers and defense attorneys have all ventured opinions, observations and assorted drivel about this mysterious creature. I think it's my turn. I am, after all, the ultimate Bundy expert.'

Before breaking off the correspondence with *The New York Times*, Bundy told Nordheimer: 'You asked why I didn't get out of town immediately after learning of the Chi Omega murders. Nothing I do can possibly be interpreted innocently, can it? If on the day after the murders, I had picked up and fled Tallahassee, you and everyone else would be asking: "Well, if you weren't guilty, why didn't you stick around, you didn't have anything to be afraid of, did you?" I didn't have anything to fear. I was not responsible for what happened at Chi Omega. I didn't do it. I wasn't there, so there was no reason for me to suspect that my presence alone would be sufficient to indict me for something I was innocent of. I am discouraged by human nature, yours included, as it applies to my case, because no matter what I say or do at this point, I am damned if I do and damned if I don't....

'Let's leave the business of proving my innocence up to me, the courts, the juries, and my defense council; and the job of finding me guilty up to the guys with the 5 o'clock shadows and the black hats. I have no illusion about convincing you or your readers that I am innocent. Let them think what they will, just as long as they don't creep on to my jury.'

Millard Farmer was unable to represent Bundy in court as he was not a member of the bar in Florida and was considered a troublemaker so, with less than two years of law school behind him, Bundy was determined to defend himself even though he was charged with several capital offences. He would, however, receive assistance from the public defender, Mike Minerva, who thought that Bundy's best chance lay in an insanity plea.

Minerva called in renowned forensic psychiatrist Doctor Emanuel Tanay, a professor at Wayne State University in Detroit and an expert in the insanity defence.

'There's no way Tanay's going to find me insane,' said Bundy.

AN EXPERT CRIMINAL PSYCHIATRIST INTERVIEWS THE 'CHIEF COUNSEL'

Before interviewing Bundy, Dr Tanay prepared the ground. He was given access to Bundy's entire file, from Sergeant Hayward's arrest report from Utah to the Florida post-mortems. In his preliminary report Dr Tanay wrote: 'The extensive interactions which Mr Bundy had with the police officers have not been carefully reviewed, however, even a

Ted Bundy finds something very amusing during a conversation with the bearded Mike Minerva in Tallahassee.

cursory perusal of that material reveals that Mr Bundy is driven by a variety of unrealistic motives such as playing games with the investigators for no other purpose than the sheer enjoyment of it. He challenges them and even taunts them. Let us assume that a psychiatrist reached the opinion that that there was a basis for insanity defense. Such a defense is not likely to prevail without some degree of cooperation of the client, who as far as I can gather from your letter rejects the insanity defense as a possibility. It is, therefore, not likely that you can persuade Mr Bundy to cooperate by logical arguments, which evidently you have tried.'

Nevertheless, Dr Tanay went on to examine Bundy.

'The interview was conducted in a conference room which was pleasant and well lighted,' Dr Tanay wrote. 'I believe there were five deputy sheriffs guarding the only exit. Mr Bundy is a 32-year-old, handsome looking man, dressed with the casual elegance of a young college professor. He was meticulously groomed from well-cared-for fingernails to freshly washed hair. He was in total command of the situation. The deputy sheriffs appeared more like a part of his entourage than policemen guarding a prisoner.

'The conference room had many comfortable chairs. Two chairs, however, were particularly comfortable looking; these were taken by the deputies into the hallway for their own use. Mr Bundy, in a very firm but definite manner, instructed the deputies that such arrangement did not meet with his approval. They not only complied with his request, but seemed to be apologetic.

'I was accompanied to the conference room by Mr Minerva, Public Defender for the Second Judicial Circuit, who has a large staff of lawyers working for him. Observing the interaction, however brief, between Mr Bundy and Mr Minerva would lead one to believe that Mr Minerva was the third assistant to Mr Bundy. Mr Bundy made a few pointed inquiries to Mr Minerva about certain work to be done and made a few polite but firm suggestions as to future work.'

Then they got down to business.

'At the outset of the interview, Mr Bundy commented on the security precautions, saying that they were the result of "the Bundy mystique", which has developed as a result of news media activities,' Dr Tanay wrote. 'This was presented in the manner of a complaint; it was, however, my impression that Mr Bundy was taking pride in his celebrity status.'

Plainly, he revelled in it.

'In the nearly three hours which I spent with Mr Bundy, I found him to be in a cheerful even jovial mood; he was witty but not flippant, he spoke freely, however, meaningful communication was never established. He was asked about his apparent lack of concern so out of keeping with the charges facing him. He acknowledged that he is facing a possible death sentence, however, "I will cross that bridge when I get to it." Mr Bundy has an incapacity to recognize the significance of evidence held against him. It would be simplistic to characterize this as merely lying inasmuch as he acts as if his perception of the significance of evidence was real. He makes decisions based upon these distorted perceptions of reality. Furthermore, he maintains an attitude and mood consistent with his perception of reality, namely, he is neither concerned nor distressed in an appropriate manner by the charges facing him.'

Dr Tanay approached the case not just as a leading forensic psychiatrist, but also as an aficionado of the legal system.

'The interactions of Mr Bundy with the police and the whole criminal justice system have been discussed at length with him and his attorneys. It is my opinion, based upon a variety of data, that his dealings with the criminal justice system are dominated by psychopathology,' Tanay said. 'Transcripts of the many hours of his conversations with police officers constitute a variety of "confession." When this is pointed out to him by me, he does not dispute my inference, he merely provides a different explanation. Whatever the explanation, the consequences of the verbal games which Mr Bundy played with investigators were counterproductive to his defense and occurred against the advice of his counsel. Mr Bundy confessed the crimes charged against him while maintaining his innocence. The intellectual denials and emotional admissions are quite apparent from the tapes and transcripts of his conversations with the investigators. This same attitude was maintained during the interview with me.'

According to Dr Tanay: 'This behavior was not, in my opinion, the result of rational reflection and decision making process but a manifestation of the psychiatric illness from which Mr Bundy suffers.'

Clearly, Bundy was enjoying the sense of power he got from being at the centre of things.

'The interview, the conference with defense counsel and the material reviewed reveal that Mr Bundy functions in the role of "a chief counsel" and the public defender has been consistently manipulated into the role of "associate counsel",' Dr Tanay continued. 'In his decision making process, Mr Bundy is guided by his emotional needs, sometimes to the detriment of his legal

Ted Bundy holds a copy of the Miami Herald *as he complains to Judge Cowart that the newspaper made him out to be a 'villain and an idiot'.*

interests. The pathological need of Mr Bundy to defy authority, to manipulate his associates and adversaries, supplies him with "thrills", to the detriment of his ability to cooperate with his counsel.

'It should be noted that Mr Bundy placed himself in a rather disadvantageous position by his non-confession. To assert the insanity defense, it is generally necessary to admit the commission of the criminal act and discuss it with defense counsel and the experts. Mr Bundy does talk to the crime investigators about "my problem" but refrains from doing so with his attorneys and the expert they have chosen.

'I realize that it could be argued that Mr Bundy has a chance to prevail on the claim of his innocence. I consider that exceedingly unlikely, not only because of the evidence which the prosecution has against him but also due to Mr Bundy's behavior in the past and in the future. I would anticipate that in the unlikely event that the prosecution's case against him would weaken, he would through his behavior bolster the prosecution's case. I have much less doubt about Mr Bundy's capacity to assist prosecution than his ability to assist his own counsel. If one assumes that his sadistic acts, including homicides, attributed to Mr Bundy in Tallahassee, were carried out by him, then psychiatrically it would be likely that various other similar acts have been perpetrated by him. It could then be argued that he is effective in concealing his criminal activities. Such an argument would be only partially true. It would be more accurate to say that he is of two minds on this issue – he attempts to conceal and reveal his involvement. He masterminds escapes with a great deal of ingenuity and arranges for his apprehension.

'In a certain sense, Mr Bundy is a producer of a play which attempts to show that various authority figures can be manipulated, set against each other and placed in positions of internal conflict. Mr Bundy does not have the capacity to recognize that the price for this "thriller" might be his own life. Mr Bundy "the super lawyer" does not recognize that his client, Bundy the defendant, is not being adequately defended.'

In the face of this expert assessment of his mental condition, Bundy dismissed any attempt to understand him on the psychological level.

For his part, Dr Tanay was stating that the insanity defence wouldn't work because Bundy wouldn't co-operate, but he also seemed to be diagnosing Bundy as a psychopath, whether or not that meant he was actually insane under US law.

'So eager is everyone, both friend and foe, to get a solid handle on my psyche that they will advance all manner of poppycock,' Bundy wrote in a letter to *The New York Times*. 'The police, for example, have purchased a lot of stock in the theory that my being born out of wedlock holds the key to the mystery – as if everyone who arrives in this world without benefit of married parents automatically qualifies as a psychopathic killer.'

In another letter he wrote: 'My response to inquiries concerning my birth without benefit of married parents is not perfunctory. It's being alive and how I am treated by those close to me that counts, and not the single physical act that resulted in my conception. I have always had a curiosity as to the identity of my biological father, but have never had the time or inclination to indulge that idle curiosity. My parents loved me and raised me, that's what matters, and this reaction of mine is hardly perfunctory. Nor is it necessary to defuse this issue, since it is not fusable in the first place. There is simply no correlation between persons who are labelled as "illegitimate" and violent behavior. But even if there were, such an explanation would not apply to me, since I have never been capable of violent behavior.'

It had already been mooted that Bundy could escape the electric chair if he made a guilty plea. In April 1979 Larry Simpson, the chief prosecutor for the Chi Omega murders, offered Minerva a plea bargain. If Bundy admitted the murders of Lisa Levy, Margaret Bowman and Kimberly Leach in open court he would receive three life sentences without possibility of parole. Judge Edward Cowart, overseeing the Chi Omega murders, agreed to the deal. So did Judge Wallace Jopling, who would preside over the Kimberly Leach murder trial. The families of the victims – including those of the victims he did not manage to kill – also agreed. Bundy would not be allowed to go back to Washington to be near his family as he wanted. On the other hand, he would not be handed over to any other state that wanted to prosecute him, where he might face the death penalty once more. Instead, he would live out his days in prison in Florida.

During their interviews Dr Tanay also raised the matter of the plea bargain with Bundy.

'I have discussed with Mr Bundy his appraisal of the evidence held against him,' he said. 'It is his view that the case against him is weak or even frivolous. This judgment of Mr Bundy's is considered to be inaccurate by his defense counsel and, most likely, represents a manifestation of his illness. In view of the fact that on conviction he faces the death sentence, the acceptance of an offer of a life sentence in exchange for a guilty plea is a consideration. This possibility seems precluded by Mr Bundy's view that the prosecution's case against him is weak. This is at least his explanation why he is unwilling to consider this particular approach. It is my impression that a major factor is his deep-seated need to have a trial, which he views as an opportunity to confront and confound various authority figures. In this last category I include, for his purposes, not only judges and prosecutors but also his defense attorneys.'

BUNDY DEMANDS HIS DAY IN COURT

Preparing his case, public defender Mike Minerva reviewed the statements Bundy had made to Florida detectives Chapman, Patchen and Bodiford. There was little possibility of keeping them out of court and they were so devastating to the defence, but Minerva did not see how they could be countered. Bundy would not accept this and grew annoyed with Minerva's insistence that the only way to save his life was to accept the plea bargain.

'I wouldn't advise a client to do this unless I thought he was culpable,' Minerva said. To Bundy, this was a betrayal. He would have no truck with anyone who thought him guilty.

Bundy would not listen to Millard Farmer either, even though he was diplomatic enough not to express an opinion on Bundy's guilt or innocence. He had come to see Bundy after John Spenkelink was executed on 25 May 1979. Spenkelink was the first convicted criminal to be put to death in Florida after capital punishment was reinstated in 1976 – the second in the US after Gary Gilmore in 1977.

Although Farmer was not allowed to appear before the Florida courts, he could take an advisory role. Farmer's advice was for Bundy to toy with the plea bargain in the hope that it would lull the prosecution into a state of complacency. Later, with the state's case in disarray, Bundy could claim that he had been forced to sign his confession under duress, then demand a trial with the prosecutors ill-prepared.

Bundy also sought the advice of John Henry Browne, his criminal defence lawyer in Washington, and contacted John

Ted Bundy in court at the Leon County sheriff's office in Florida shortly after his arrest on a charge of theft. He did not perhaps understand the full implications of the charges he faced.

O'Connell, his attorney in Salt Lake City, telling him that representing himself gave him peace of mind.

'It also gives me things like phone calls, a typewriter, law books, and other considerations which foaming-at-the-mouth, bloodthirsty, escape-prone monsters don't receive,' he said.

As far as Millard Farmer was concerned, with Bundy defending himself the verdict was a forgone conclusion. He told *The New York Times*: 'The only reason for the trial is to let him try and prove beyond reasonable doubt that he isn't a murderer, which isn't possible. All the state needs to prove him guilty is to read the indictment in court.' In effect, he had already been convicted and sentenced to death.

On the advice of Farmer, Bundy's mother Louise and his girlfriend Carole Boone travelled from Washington State to urge him to sign the plea bargain agreement. Carole was now more in love with Bundy than ever. With the help of a compliant prison guard, they seized the opportunity to consummate their relationship. It seems Bundy also got hold of some pills and was high next time he appeared in court.

On 30 May 1979 the lawyers appeared in court, saying that they had a verbal agreement from Bundy. The following morning the court was full. Sheriff Ken Katsaris was accused of packing the courtroom, but apparently news had got around that Bundy was going to confess. It seems he had written a confession, but his aim was to take his revenge on Mike Minerva, who arrived in court to find Bundy distributing a motion asking for the removal of Minerva and the rest of the defence team, saying they were ill-prepared and had adopted a 'defeatist posture'.

Carole Boone pictured in court when she was pregnant in 1979; her condition prompted questions about prison security during visiting hours.

During a brief recess Millard Farmer told Bundy: 'Well, Ted, we really gave it a try here. I've got no hard feelings, but I've only got so much time and I'm going to spend it on people who want to live.'

Nevertheless, Farmer thought there was still a 50–50 chance he would agree to the plea bargain when they went back into the courtroom. Mike Minerva had no idea either and merely announced: 'Mr Bundy has a matter to present to the court.'

Bundy then presented his motion asking for Minerva and the defence team to be removed.

'Your Honour, it is not simply my point of view that I'm not receiving effectiveness of counsel,' he said. 'It is my position that my counsel, one, believe that I'm guilty; two, that they have told me they see no way of presenting an effective defence, and in no uncertain terms they have told me that; and three, that they see no way of avoiding conviction. Now, Your Honour, if this doesn't raise itself to the level of ineffectiveness of counsel, I don't know what does.'

'The prosecutors waited until he finished,' said Minerva. 'When he had completed his motion attacking us and asking us to be released, then he sort of looked at me and sat down. We had a little whispered discussion – he seemed to want to enter a plea now that he'd gotten this off his chest – and the prosecutors sat down at the table and said no deal, it's off.'

They weren't about to give Bundy the legal argument that he had been inadequately defended, which could have undermined the validity of his confessions later.

This meant that the trials for the Chi Omega murders and for the murder of Kimberly Leach would both go ahead. The defence team were demoralized.

'It took all the wind out of our sails, what little wind we had left,' said Minerva. 'We had become quite emotionally involved in the case. We were pretty well exhausted.'

Carole Boone was upset too, believing that the plea bargain

Ted Bundy leans against the wall as an indictment charging him with the murder of two FSU co-eds at the Chi Omega house is read out by Leon County Sheriff Ken Katarsis.

was Bundy's only chance of escaping the electric chair. On the plane back to Seattle, she wrote to him, saying: 'Poops, check to see if you are part of the problem.'

Judge Cowart found no merit in Bundy's argument that his defence team was incompetent, but Mike Minerva was allowed to withdraw from the case. However, he had one last throw of the dice and was granted a hearing to determine whether Bundy was competent to stand trial.

Dr Tanay was called and told the court that he believed Bundy suffered from a mental disorder. The prosecution's psychiatrist, Dr Hervey Cleckley, a leading authority on psycho-paths, confirmed Dr Tanay's diagnosis. But Bundy refused to co-operate. He insisted that he was both sane and innocent, and demanded his case go to trial. Judge Cowart had little option but to find him competent.

Warming to his role as an attorney, Bundy then sued Sheriff Katsaris in a $300,000 civil suit for depriving him of adequate light, exercise and access to the press. Sheriff Katsaris had to use $7,000 of his own money to defend himself. Meanwhile, Bundy got a letter to a reporter from Denver's *Rocky Mountain News* saying: 'I have killed no one. Outside a few minor thefts, I have done nothing wrong. What the media reports now is completely one-sided, nothing but accusation and insinuation – spoon-fed by the investigative authorities.'

In his pre-trial role as his own attorney Bundy was allowed to take depositions from numerous policemen and laboratory technicians. He was also able to compel sisters from the Chi Omega sorority to visit him in jail and answer questions about the night of the attack. Even Karen Chandler, who had been grievously wounded, would be forced to appear.

CHAPTER TEN

Not Suitable for Children

ON 12 JUNE Judge Cowart granted a change of venue from Tallahassee to Miami, where the trial began on 25 June 1979. Over the objections of the defence, television cameras were allowed in the courtroom. A 30-minute digest of the highlights was broadcast in Colorado, Utah and Washington State, along with other major metropolitan TV markets, prefaced with the warning that the content 'May not be suitable viewing for children'.

Time and *Newsweek* carried stories on the trial and some two hundred reporters descended on the courtroom. Carole Boone was on hand for photographs, interviews and to provide selective access to her 'Bunny'. She had been fired from her job in state government for backing Bundy and arrived in Miami with her teenage son Jamey, where they were surviving on the munificence of journalists. Her aim was to present her boyfriend in a favourable light and insisted that she would not believe he was guilty until the prosecution produced some irrefutable physical evidence.

Bundy had a young defence team that he manipulated. This did little to help his case. He also went head-to-head with Judge Cowart, who agreed to delay the start of the trial for one day so Bundy could prepare more. He also allowed a new desk, better lighting in his cell and access to the law library. They fell out when Bundy violated a gagging order, telling reporters: 'The final decision on all jurors is up to me. That is the way it should be.'

After that, Judge Cowart ordered that Bundy be manacled and returned to the cells during every recess.

The selection of the jury took five days. The panel comprised five women – one white, one Latina and three African American – and seven men – three white and four African American. Three alternates were selected, but these were quickly used up. As the jury was going to be sequestered for several weeks, two jurors were allowed to leave because of family commitments, while one young woman was discharged because she said she found Bundy scary.

However, there were a number of young women in the courtroom who did not. Some passed him notes making lewd suggestions. Ann Rule, who was in the press box, wondered whether they knew how much they resembled his victims.

For the first few days the jury remained sequestered in a plush hotel on Biscayne Bay, while Judge Cowart heard preliminary arguments. The defence wanted the testimony of Nita Neary excluded, arguing that her identification of Bundy as the man she had seen in the Chi Omega sorority house on the night of the attacks was inadmissible because her mother had shown her newspaper pictures of Bundy after he had been arrested. For the prosecution Nita was vital because she was their only eyewitness. Badgered by the defence, she was soon on the verge of tears. However, asked if she saw the man she had seen fleeing the sorority house with a club in the courtroom, she said: 'Yes, I believe I do.'

As she had only seen the suspect that night in profile, Judge Cowart asked every man in the court to stand and turn sideways. She pointed at Bundy and Judge Cowart ruled that her testimony was admissible. He would also admit the testimony of forensic odontologist (dentist) Doctor Richard Souviron over the objections of the defence. He would match Bundy's bite to the teeth marks on Lisa Levy's buttocks.

However, Judge Cowart would not allow the testimony of Sergeant Hayward and Deputy Ondrak, ruling that Bundy's arrest in Utah was too remote from the matters before the court. Nor would the jury be allowed to hear that a pantyhose mask similar to the one found in Cheryl Thomas' apartment had been impounded from Bundy's VW Beetle three years earlier.

The tapes made by Detectives Chapman and Patchen were also ruled inadmissible as the tape recorder had regularly been turned off, albeit at Bundy's request, therefore they did not comprise a complete record of the interview. No mention could be made of Bundy's talk of feeling 'like a vampire', his admission of voyeurism and doing 'the act' to keep his fantasies alive. To the prosecution this was a disaster, and the feeling among the press was that Bundy was now in with a fighting chance.

With the pre-trial arguments out of the way, the trial proper started on 7 July, but the defence said they were still not ready.

'We need time between your rulings and our opening statement,' said 29-year-old Margaret Good, an appellate, or appeals, specialist who was heading Bundy's team but who had never tried a felony case – that is, an offence punishable by death or a prison sentence of more than one year. 'We're exhausted, we've only had five hours sleep a night. You're turning this into a trial by endurance.'

Fifty-three-year-old Judge Cowart would have none of it.

'You have four lawyers in Miami, one investigator, two law students helping you,' he said. 'I'm very satisfied that there is no reason to delay any further. In this circuit, it's not unusual to proceed until midnight. We vary the tune, but we've got the same fiddler, the same music. Every minute you've been here, I've been here – and I'm as fresh as a daisy.'

Bundy pitched in.

'I'm concerned about Your Honour,' he said. 'How you're going to get this done by one o'clock?'

It was noon on a Saturday and the court closed at one. Bundy wanted to start fresh on Monday morning. Judge Cowart did not.

'You just watch us,' he said. 'I appreciate your concern.'

'My attorneys are not ready,' insisted Bundy.

'We will begin, Mr Bundy,' said Judge Cowart.

'Then you'll start without me, Your Honour,' Bundy said in pique.

'As you like,' said Judge Cowart.

The jury was brought in and chief prosecutor Larry Simpson began his opening statement. On a blackboard he listed the charges and the victims' names. There was the first degree murder of Lisa Levy and Margaret Bowman, and the first degree attempted murder of Kathy Kleiner, Karen Chandler and Cheryl Thomas, along with the burglary of the Chi Omega sorority house and Cheryl Thomas' apartment on Dunwoody Street – that is, entering these buildings illegally with the intent of committing a crime, even though nothing was taken.

THE DEFENCE LIMPS OFF THE BLOCKS

Thirty-four-year-old Robert Haggard, a Miami attorney who had been on the case just two weeks, was selected by Bundy to open for the defence. Judge Cowart advised him to wait until the prosecution case had been heard before making his opening statement, but Haggard went ahead anyway. During his 26-minute opening speech the prosecution objected 29 times – 23 of these were sustained. It was not a good start for the defence.

Bundy himself led the cross-examination of Officer Ray Crew, who had discovered Lisa Levy's dead body. Bundy was seen to relish every detail he elicited, almost as if he had been there and was now gloating over what he had done.

'Describe the condition of Lisa Levy's room,' he asked.

'Clothing strewn about, desk, books... some disarray,' said Officer Crew.

'Any blood in any area in the room other than what you testified about earlier?'

'No sir.'

Officer Crew had also been into Margaret Bowman's room that night.

'Describe the condition of Margaret Bowman's body,' said Bundy.

'She was lying face down, mouth and eyes open. Nylon stocking knotted around her neck, head bloated and discoloured,' Crew said. Bundy sought to show that the officer had not proceeded with due care and had left fingerprints all over the evidence. All he succeeded in doing was painting a vivid picture of the horrific crime scene.

The jury was shown piles of bloody clothes and bedding, the Clairol bottle used to sodomize Lisa Levy and the pantyhose ligature found around Margaret Bowman's neck, along with the pantyhose mask found in Cheryl Thomas' apartment.

VICTIMS AND WITNESSES STEP UP BRAVELY IN COURT

This gruesome evidence was followed by the testimony of young women from the sorority house – Melanie Nelson, Nancy Young, Nancy Dowdy, Debbie Ciccarelli, Karen Chandler and Kathy Kleiner. There were no outward signs that Karen and Kathy had been injured. Pins held their jaws together and their other wounds had long since healed. Nevertheless, they described the injuries they had suffered, never once looking at Bundy.

Cheryl Thomas had not recovered though, and limped into the courtroom. Sitting on the witness chair, she had to

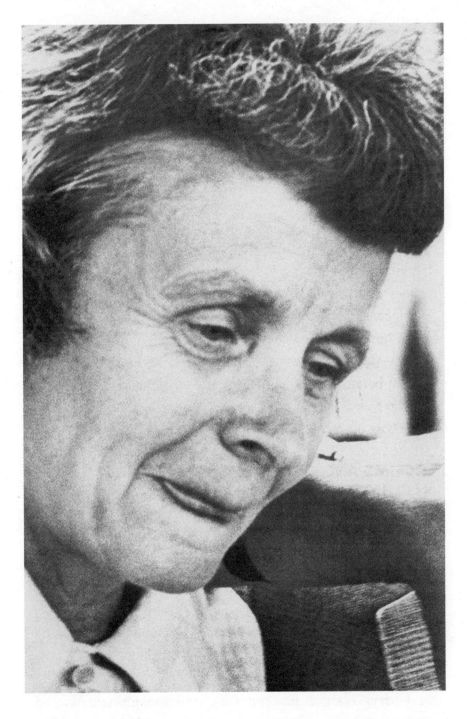

Ted Bundy's mother Louise leaving the Dade County Courthouse, Miami.

turn her head so that her right ear was towards the prosecutor so she could hear. The attack had left her completely deaf in the left ear.

'I had five skull fractures and multiple contusions to the head,' she said. 'The eighth [cranial] nerve was damaged and I lost the hearing of my left ear and equilibrium. And I had a broken jaw and my left shoulder was pulled out of joint.'

The defence chose not to cross-examine her.

Dr Thomas Wood testified about the post-mortems he conducted on Lisa Levy and Margaret Bowman. He introduced 11 in by 14 in (28 cm by 36 cm) colour photographs of their bodies. Defence attorney Margaret Good objected, saying they were 'inflammatory and with no probative value.' They were admitted anyway.

There were pictures of Lisa Levy's right breast with the nipple bitten through, her bludgeoned face and the bite mark on her buttocks. Judge Cowart called one of the close-ups of Margaret Bowman 'the hole-in-the-head picture', as the blow had been so traumatic. One of the women in the jury almost vomited at the sight. The men paled and winced.

Robert Fulford, the manager of The Oaks rooming house, was brought in to testify about Bundy's disappearance from Tallahassee, telling of his first contact with the man he knew as 'Chris Hagen' when Fulford rented him a room with a bunk bed, desk, table and chest of drawers.

'He didn't have the rent when it came due,' Fulford said. 'He said he could call his mother long distance in Wisconsin and she'd send it down. I heard him make the call, and it seemed like he was talking to someone, but he never showed up with the rent. When I checked his room a couple of days later, he was gone.'

Patrolman David Lee testified about Bundy's arrest in Pensacola. He told the jury that Bundy had said he wanted to die.

The following day, 17 July, Bundy did not appear in the packed courtroom. The jury was sequestered and Bundy's jailer, Sergeant Marty Kratz, was called. He told Judge Cowart that Bundy had caused trouble that night. At around 1 am he had thrown an orange through the bars of his cell, smashing a light that had been installed outside the door to give him better illumination. Bundy was moved to the next cell, while the first cell was searched. Broken glass from the smashed light bulb was found. It was not clear if he intended to use this to commit suicide, or in an attempt to escape.

When the guards came to get Bundy in the morning, Sergeant Kratz said, they could not get the key in the lock. He had jammed it with lavatory paper. He was then reminded that he was due in court at 9 am.

'I'll be there when I feel like it,' he said.

Judge Cowart found Bundy in contempt of court for using delaying tactics and sent his lawyers to get him. When Bundy appeared at 9.30 am he complained of his treatment. He had been denied access to the law library and proper exercise. Files had also been withheld, he said, his voice cracking, on the verge of tears.

'There comes a time when the only thing I can do is passively resist,' he said. 'I have potential. Now I have only used part of my potential which is nonviolent. There comes a time when I have to say: "Whoa…"'

'Whoa?' said Judge Cowart. 'If you say "Whoa," I'm going to have to use spurs.'

Bundy listed his grievances, wagging a finger at Judge Cowart.

'Don't shake a finger at me, young man,' said the judge.

Bundy turned towards the defence table.

'That's fine,' said Judge Cowart. 'You can shake it at Mr Haggard.'

Bundy agreed.

'He probably deserves it better than you do,' Bundy said. 'In the three weeks I've been here I've been taken to the law library three times.'

'On at least three occasions you've just sat up there and talked to Sergeant Kratz,' said the judge. 'You never used the library itself.'

'That's not true,' said Bundy. 'It is a joke, but it's a better place to read than the interview room. There is no justification for the treatment I'm receiving. I am given a strip search after I see my attorney and that is unconscionable. Now, the railroad train is running, but if I'm going to get off, I'll get off if I need to demonstrate to this courtroom that they are influencing me and affecting me.'

Judge Cowart was clear he would brook no more trouble from Bundy.

'This court is going to proceed on schedule without your voluntary interruptions,' he said. 'We're not going to have any more. Now I want you to discuss that with your counsel. I want you to know your rights, but I also want you to know that as forbearing as this court can be it can also be strong.'

'I'm willing to accept the consequences of my actions, Your Honour,' said Bundy, 'and anything I do I'm aware of what the court will do.'

'Then we're together,' said Judge Cowart. 'Bless your heart, and I just hope you stay with us. If you don't, we'll miss you.'

Looking around the crowded courtroom, Bundy said: 'And all these people won't pay their money to come and see me.'

Microanalyst Patricia Lasko then testified that two hairs found in the pantyhose mask in Cheryl Thomas's flat were 'from Mr Bundy or from someone whose hair is exactly like his.'

Haggard badgered the witness, then grabbed her notebook. Prosecutor Larry Simpson then tried to grab it from Haggard's hand and a tug-of-war ensued. Judge Cowart censured the two men. The jury was sent out and he said to Simpson: 'It's the first time I've seen you get your dander up.'

Nita Neary was then called. She raised her arm again to identify Bundy as the man she had seen fleeing the sorority house – this time in front of the jury. Testimony on semen found at the scene was also given. Before DNA testing, it was only possible to detect the blood type of the man the sperm had come from.

VITAL BITE MARK EVIDENCE HURTS BUNDY

Until the murders at Chi Omega Bundy had been a cunning criminal. He rarely left any physical evidence that connected him to the crime. But in the Chi Omega murders, the teeth marks left on Lisa Levy's buttocks proved crucial. Forensic odontologist Dr Richard Souviron told the jury: 'No two grains of sand are alike and no two fingerprints are alike. The same is true about teeth.'

He produced a picture of Bundy's teeth in Leon County Jail, taken after a warrant had been served. He superimposed this on to a picture of the bite mark on Lisa Levy's buttocks, showing the images lined up exactly. In fact, the purple teeth marks on the buttocks showed a double bite.

'The individual bit once, then turned sideways and bit a second time,' said Dr Souviron. 'The top teeth stayed in about the same position, but the lower teeth – biting harder – left two rings.'

This made identification easier, said Dr Souviron, as he had twice as much to work with. 'They line up perfectly, exactly – it is convincing beyond any discussion whatsoever. I'm not saying that this set of teeth killed anybody. I'm saying that these teeth made those marks.'

'Doctor,' asked Simpson. 'Based on your analysis and comparison of this particular bite mark, can you tell us within a reasonable degree of dental certainty whether or not the teeth represented in that photograph as being those of Theodore Robert Bundy and the teeth represented by the models that have been introduced as state's exhibits number 85, 86, made the bite marks reflecting on your exhibit as marked and admitted to evidence?'

'Yes, sir,' said Dr Souviron.

'And what is that opinion?' asked the prosecutor.

'They made the marks,' said Dr Souviron.

The court erupted. For the first time a piece of clear physical evidence linked Bundy to one of his victims. It was then vital for the defence to show that the science of forensic odontology was in its infancy and could not offer such certainty beyond reasonable doubt.

The 29-year-old defence lawyer Ed Harvey began his cross-examination by saying: 'Analyzing bite marks is part art and part science, isn't it?'

'I think that's a fair statement,' said Dr Souviron.

'And that it really depends on the experience and education of the examiner?'

'Yes.'

'And your conclusions are really a matter of opinion. Is that correct?'

'That is correct.'

'You've got a given set of teeth, or models, and a given area of skin, a thigh or a calf. Is there any way to test whether those teeth will make the same marks over and over?' asked Harvey.

'Yes, because I did an experiment just like that,' said Dr Souviron with a smile. 'I took models and I went to the morgue and I pressed the models into the buttocks area on different individuals and photographed them. Yes, they can be standardized, and, yes, they do match.'

'You said cadavers. Is that correct?' said Harvey, with feigned incredulity.

'I couldn't find any live volunteers,' Dr Souviron explained. 'If there's an area of inconsistency – out it goes. If there's a Vee'd-out central that wouldn't make this pattern, you'd say: "Well, we'll have to exclude that person even though the arch size is the same, the cuspids are tucked down in behind the laterals and this type of thing. The centrals don't line up right." The odds of finding this would be a needle in a haystack – an identical set like Mr Bundy's – with the wear on the centrals and everything, the chipped lateral incisor, everything identical. You'd have to be able to combine that with the three marks on the upper central incisors, and the odds against that are astronomical.'

Finally, the prosecution called Dr Lowell J. Levine, the Chief Consultant in Forensic Dentistry to the New York City Medical Examiner. He testified that he believed Lisa Levy – or at least the person whose flesh appeared in the photograph he studied – had been 'passive' when the bite marks were left on her body.

'There is very little evidence of motion or swirling you'd normally get as tissue moves in various directions as the teeth move on the skin,' he said. 'It almost looks more like an animal which has bitten and kinda grabs. These things were left slowly, and the person was not moving. They were passive when they were left.'

'Can you give us an opinion as to the uniqueness of teeth?' asked Simpson.

'Everybody's teeth are unique to that particular person for a number of reasons. One, the shapes of the teeth are unique, in addition to the juxtaposition or the relationship of each tooth to the other is unique, the twisting or tipping or bending also

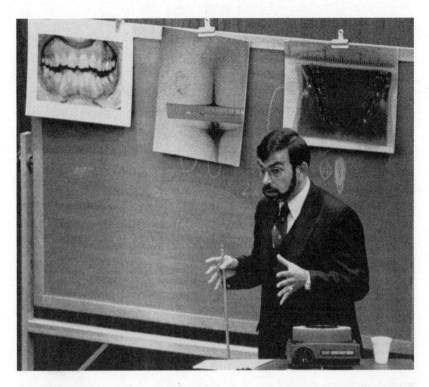

Dr Lowell J. Levine, a New York ondontologist, testified that there was a high degree of probability that the bite marks found on the buttock of co-ed Lisa Levy came from Bundy's teeth, pictured top left.

adds to that uniqueness,' said Dr Levine. 'Present and missing teeth and those are basically gross characteristics. We also have other types of individual characteristics which are accidental characteristics, such as breaking.'

Mike Minerva had rejoined the defence team to cross-examine Dr Levine.

'When you say "reasonable degree of dental certainty" you are speaking of some kind of probability. Is that right?' he asked.

'A very high degree of probability. Yes sir,' said Dr Levine.

Again, Minerva sought to undermine any faith the jury may have put in these experts.

'Would you say that it is fair to say that odontology is a relatively new, newly recognized forensic science?' he asked. But Dr Levine would have none of it.

'No. I do not think that is fair at all. Historically, you have a case of Paul Revere doing identifications.' The American revolutionary identified the body of his friend Joseph Warren, nine months after he had been killed at the Battle of Bunker Hill, from his teeth.

'You have testimony admitted to the bar in Massachusetts in the late 1800s on identification,' Dr Levine went on, 'and you can find citations for bite mark cases even in the legal justice system that go back 25 years. So what's new?'

After the prosecution rested its case, Bundy asked that Dr Souviron be held in contempt of court for speaking out about the case at a seminar in Orlando before the trial. Judge Cowart denied his request. Then, as the courtroom emptied, Bundy studied the dental exhibits of his teeth and the pictures of Lisa Levy's bite marks. This was the crucial piece of evidence that would convict him and he knew it.

The defence team were now in disarray. Haggard insisted that Bundy's questioning of Officer Crew had been a mistake and quit. When the case for the defence opened on 20 July, Bundy rose again to argue that his defence team were inadequate.

ANGRY AND IN CONTEMPT OF COURT

'I did not have any choice in the selection of Bob Haggard to represent me here in Miami,' he complained. 'In total, I have not been asked at any time my opinion about who should be representing me within the public defender's office.'

It wasn't just Haggard. Bundy had little time for any of the lawyers allocated to him.

'I think it's also important to note that there are certain problems of communication between myself and my attorneys which have reduced my defence – the defence which is not my defence or sanctioned by me, nor one which I can say I agree with,' said Bundy.

He complained that his lawyers ignored his input into the case, would not let him make decisions and refused to allow him to cross-examine further witnesses before the jury. But Judge Cowart had little time for his grousing.

'I don't know of any case I've seen or experienced where an individual who is indigent has received the quality and quantity of counsel you have,' he pointed out. 'There have been five separate counsel here representing you. It's unheard of. Who's minding the store for the public defender I can't tell you. And what's happening to all those other indigents they represent I can't tell you. This court has watched with a great deal of carefulness that, before witnesses are tendered, you are questioned, and this record will show hundreds of "just a moment, pleases" where they go by and confer with you. I've never seen anything like it in the history of any case I've ever tried. Or in 27 years at the bar have I ever seen anything exactly like what has happened in the defence of this case.'

Fool for a Client

HAVING LEARNED NOTHING from his conviction in Utah, once again Bundy insisted on discharging his attorneys and conducting his own defence. Judge Cowart agreed to allow this, but cited the old saying that a lawyer who represents himself has a fool for a client.

'I've always taken that particular axiom like someone who works on his own car has a fool for a mechanic,' said Bundy. 'It all depends on how much you want to do by yourself.'

While Bundy would now be in charge of his own defence, Judge Cowart ruled that his attorneys should stay on, but their role would be reduced to that of advisors.

'If they don't do every little, single, solitary thing that you want them to, they're incompetent. And, bless your heart, if they do I'm gonna fire them,' said Judge Cowart. However, he said that they had been to law school and had passed their bar exams.

'I can't conceive of submitting myself, or I'm sure you wouldn't submit yourself, to brain surgery by somebody who had only a year and a half of medical school,' he said, disparaging Bundy's lack of training.

The problem was that Bundy had no alibi and Ed Harvey admitted, out of the hearing of the jury, that the defence was a shambles. He wanted to quit too. But first he had one last shot at saving his client. He asked for another competency hearing.

'The man's life is at stake,' said Harvey. 'He shouldn't be forced to take the services of public lawyers whom he has no confidence in. His conduct has revealed the debilitating effects of his mental disorder by reflecting a total lack of insight regarding the disorder and its effects on him, by reflecting a wholly inadequate ability to consult with lawyers about the case.'

Prosecutor Larry Simpson's assistant Danny McKeever opposed the competency motion.

'The man is difficult to work with,' he argued. 'He's almost cunning the way he works against his attorneys sometimes, but he's competent.'

This brought a smile to Bundy's face. Judge Cowart found that Bundy was competent too, and worked out a compromise as the trial was now nearing its end. Ed Harvey would stay on. Fellow Leon County public defender Lynn Thompson would stay on too, while Margaret Good would make the final arguments. Bundy was pleased with this arrangement.

'I feel really, really, good,' he said later.

CHIP OR NO CHIP?

The defence then called Doctor Duane DeVore, Professor of Oral Surgery at the University of Maryland and an advisor in forensic dentistry to the chief medical examiner of the state of Maryland. He testified that while teeth themselves are unique, bite marks are not necessarily so.

'The material of skin is flexible, elastic, and, depending upon the bleeding structures underneath and the amount of blood, a tooth may not leave a unique mark,' he said.

Dr DeVore produced four models of teeth from Maryland youngsters which he said could have caused the bite marks. Under cross-examination he admitted that Bundy's teeth also could have made the same marks.

The defence then produced a tape of Nita Neary under hypnosis. On it she said that the Chi Omega worker, Ronnie Eng, had resembled the intruder. Eng was brought into the courtroom and stood beside Bundy for the jury to make their own comparison.

Serologist Michael J. Grubb, of the Institute of Forensic Sciences in Oakland, testified that the semen left on Cheryl Thomas' sheet could not have come from Bundy. However, his scientific argument was long and intricate and seemed to confuse the jury.

Bundy tried to introduce photographic evidence that a chip on one of his front teeth that Dr Souviron had identified had not been there when the Chi Omega attacks took place. However, his investigator Joe Aloi had not been able to obtain negatives of photographs shown in the newspapers so he could enlarge them. Instead, Bundy took to the witness stand.

Under questioning by defence counsel Margaret Good, Bundy testified that his tooth had been chipped in the middle of March 1978, two months after the murders in Tallahassee.

'I recall I was eating dinner in my cell in the Leon County Jail and I bit down hard, just like you bite down on a rock or pebble, and I pulled it out and it was just a white piece of tooth, and it just chipped out of one of my central incisors,' he said.

Danny McKeever began his cross-examination for the prosecution.

'You don't know what the Utah dental records look like, do you?' he asked.

'I've never seen the dental records themselves,' said Bundy

'Would you be surprised to know that those teeth appear to be chipped from the Utah dental records?'

'Yes, I would,' Bundy replied.

McKeever produced the records to prove his point. Bundy countered by calling Carole Boone, who had visited him in the Garfield County Jail in Colorado in late 1977.

'Did you visit me there? How many times?' he asked.

'I don't have my records with me, but I believe I visited with you on six or seven consecutive days, both in the morning and the afternoon,' she said. 'On a few afternoons, we visited in the law library in the courthouse and then we would walk back together to the jail, about half a block.'

She testified that, to the best of her memory, Bundy had no chip at all in his front tooth at that time.

Bundy then called for a halt in proceedings while subpoenas were issued that would force all newspapers to turn over their negatives.

'I think you'd understand what I'm getting at,' Bundy told Judge Cowart. 'If that chip did not occur until March 1978, a month or two after the Chi Omega crimes, and if the state's odontologists say that space between the two linear abrasions could only have been made by a tooth with a chip or a gap between the two central incisors, then there's obviously something wrong with the observations made by the state's odontologists. Our contention all along, Your Honour, is that they have taken my teeth and twisted them every which way but loose to fit.'

Judge Cowart was unmoved. He ruled that this was no time to introduce new evidence about the defendant's teeth. There would be no subpoenas. When Bundy moved to reopen the issue, Judge Cowart said: 'Mr Bundy, you may jump up and down, hang from the chandelier, do anything you want to, but the court has ruled and the case is closed.'

Bundy mumbled some derogatory statements under his breath.

'You impress me not, sir,' the judge admonished.

'Well, I suppose the feeling is mutual, Your Honour,' Bundy replied.

Again Judge Cowart refused to rise to the bait.

'I'm sure it is, bless your heart,' he said.

CLOSING ARGUMENTS

Larry Simpson then made the closing arguments for the prosecution, speaking for about 40 minutes.

'First-degree murder can be committed in the state of Florida in two different ways,' he explained. 'It can be done by a person who premeditates and thinks about what he's going to do and then goes out and does it. That's exactly what the evidence showed in this particular case: a premeditated, a brutal murder of two young girls sleeping in their beds. The second way is during the commission of a burglary. The state has proved a burglary in this case.

'I asked Nita Neary the question, on the witness stand: "Nita, do you recall the man you saw at the door of the Chi Omega sorority house the morning of January 15, 1978?" Her exact words were: "Yes, sir. I do." I asked her: "Nita, is that man in the courtroom today?" She said: "Yes, sir. He is." And she pointed him out. That in and of itself is proof of this defendant's guilt, and it is sufficient to support a conviction in this case.

'In Sherrod's, Mary Ann Picano also saw the man. He scared her so bad she can't even remember what he looked like. He came up to her and asked her to dance. What were the words Mary Ann Picano used to her friend when she went to dance with the man? She said: "I think I'm about to dance with an ex-con... " Ladies and gentlemen, this man was next door to the Chi Omega sorority house the morning of the murders and there was something wrong with him!'

Simpson continued to go through the circumstantial evidence. There was the testimony of Rusty Gage and Henry

Palumbo of The Oaks, that they had seen 'Chris Hagen' standing at the front door of the rooming house just after the attacks, looking back toward the campus.

'They told you that the defendant in this case said to them that he thought this was a professional job – a professional job – done by somebody who had done it before and was probably long gone,' said Simpson. 'Ladies and gentlemen, this man recognized from the morning of these murders that this was a professional job, that no clues had been left. He thought he'd gotten away scot-free.'

Simpson drew attention to the licence plate stolen from Randy Regan's van, the theft of the Volkswagen Beetle, the escape to Pensacola, and the room wiped clean of prints and left empty of all possessions.

'He had loaded up and packed up everything he had, and he was getting out of Dodge,' said Simpson. 'That's what it amounts to. The heat was on and he was going.'

Then there was Patrolman David Lee's arrest of Bundy in Pensacola.

'Theodore Robert Bundy said to him: "I wish you had killed me. If I run now, will you shoot me?" Why did he say those things to Officer Lee?' asked Simpson. 'Here is a man that has created, committed, the most horrible and brutal murders known to the Tallahassee area. That's why. He can't live with himself anymore and he wants Officer Lee to kill him right there.'

Simpson turned to the forensic evidence. Microanalyst Patricia Lasko's testimony linked the two curly brown hairs in the pantyhose mask beside Cheryl Thomas' bed to those on Ted Bundy's head.

'That pantyhose mask came directly from the man that committed these crimes,' he said. 'The hairs from that pantyhose mask also came from that man.'

For Simpson, though, Dr Souviron's testimony was the clincher.

'What was his conclusion?' he asked. 'With a reasonable degree of dental certainty, Theodore Robert Bundy made that bite mark in the body of Lisa Levy. Asked in cross-examination about the possibility of someone else in the world having teeth that could have left those marks, what did he say? He said it would be like finding a needle in a haystack.

'When Dr Levine was asked about the possibility of someone else leaving this bite mark, or someone else having teeth that could leave this bite mark, he told you it was a practical impossibility. A practical impossibility.'

Simpson ended by pointing out the desperation of the defence when confronted with this vital evidence.

'On cross-examination, Dr DeVore, the defence expert, had to tell you, and did, that the defendant, Theodore Robert Bundy, could have left that bite mark,' he said.

'Ladies and gentlemen,' he continued, 'the defence was in a real problem situation. Anytime they've got to put a witness on who will say that their man could have committed this crime, they've got real problems. And it was a desperate move – a damned desperate move that might have succeeded – but did not.'

It was then Margaret Good's turn to speak for the defence. But she had almost nothing to work with – just the equivocal evidence of two expert witnesses against the testimony of 49 prosecution witnesses and the 100 exhibits. She could only fall back on an appeal to 'reasonable doubt'.

'The defence is not denying there was a great and horrible tragedy that occurred in Tallahassee on 15 January,' said Good. 'True, that these four unfortunate women were beaten while sleeping in their beds – injured, killed. But I ask you not to compound that tragedy by convicting the wrong man when the state's evidence is insufficient to prove beyond a reasonable doubt that Mr Bundy, and no one else, is the person that committed these crimes. How tragic it would be if a man's life could be taken from him because 12 people thought he was probably guilty, but they were not sure. You must assure yourself that you will not wake up and doubt your decision and wonder if you convicted the wrong man here two weeks after he is dead and gone.'

She tried to find fault with the police investigation.

'There are basically two ways for the police to investigate a crime,' she said. 'They can go to the crime scene, they can look for the clues, and they can follow the clues to their logical conclusions and find a suspect. Or they can find the suspect, decide on the suspect, and decide to make the evidence fit the suspect and work to make the evidence fit only him.'

She attacked the prosecution's presentation of its case, criticizing the introduction of bloody sheets and gruesome photographs to the courtroom, the mishandling of evidence and the lack of fingerprints. Good even cast doubt on the eyewitness identification, particularly that of Nita Neary.

'She wants to help if she can,' said Good. 'And she can't let herself believe that the man who committed these crimes is still out on the street.'

The fact that Bundy left Tallahassee after the murders was not an admission of guilt, she contended.

'There are lots of reasons a person might run from the cops,' she said. 'One reason is that you might be afraid you'd be railroaded. You might be afraid you'd be charged with something you didn't do. It's clear Mr Bundy left town because he was out of money. He was running out on the rent.'

Dealing with the key testimonies of Dr Souviron and Dr Levine, she said that the investigators had found Bundy and matched his teeth to the bite marks, rather than searching for the person who had actually made the bite.

'If you want to convict on the best shell in a confidence game, maybe you'll accept what Souviron and Levine have to say. It will be a sad day for our system of justice if a man can be convicted in our courts on the quality of the state's evidence, and you can put a man's life on the line because they say he has crooked teeth, without any proof that such are unique, without any scientific facts or data to base their conclusions.'

It was then Larry Simpson's turn to come back with rebuttal.

'Ladies and gentlemen, the man who committed this crime was smart,' he said. 'This man premeditated this murder. He knew what he was going to do before he did it, and planned it, and prepared himself for it. If there is any question in your mind about that, just look at the pantyhose mask. That is a weapon that was prepared by the perpetrator of this crime. Now, ladies and gentlemen, somebody took the time to make this weapon right here, this instrument that could be used for both – a mask that could hide identity or also for strangulation.

'Anybody who took the time to do that is not going to leave fingerprints at a crime scene. And there was not a single fingerprint in room 12 at The Oaks. The room had been wiped clean.

'Ladies and gentlemen, this man is a professional, just as he told Rusty Gage at The Oaks back in January 1978. He's the kind of a man smart enough to stand in the courtroom and move to the end of the banister and cross-examine witnesses in this case because he thinks he is smart enough to get away with any crime, just like he told Rusty Gage.'

Bundy himself contributed nothing at this stage. He sat quietly at the defence table, sometimes staring at his hands, as if to draw attention to the fact that they did not appear particularly powerful.

THE VERDICT: 'IT'S TOO SOON'

The jurors retired at 2.57 pm on 23 July. When they had not come up with a verdict after an hour's deliberation, Bundy was returned to his cell in the Dade County Jail. Meanwhile, reporters were betting on the outcome. The odds given were evens. Bundy's mother Louise, his girlfriend Carole Boone and her son Jamey awaited news of his fate. Few doubted that if Bundy was convicted, he would be given the death penalty.

While awaiting his fate, Bundy was composed enough to give an interview by phone.

'Is it just being in the wrong place at the wrong time?' the reporter asked.

'It's just being Ted Bundy in any place, I guess, anymore,' he said. 'It started out in Utah and it seemed like one set of circumstances seemed to bootstrap another, to feed on one another, and once you get people thinking in that vein… police officers, they want to solve crimes, and I sometimes don't think they really think things through. They're willing to take the convenient alternative. The convenient alternative is me.'

He clung to the belief that James Bennett, a 43-year-old truck driver on the jury, was sympathetic to the defence. He was also cheered by reports that laughter had been heard emanating from the jury room – on the grounds that laughing juries do not convict.

At 3.50 pm, the jurors sent out for pencils and legal pads. They returned to the courtroom at 6.30 pm with a question for Judge Cowart. They wanted to know if the two curly brown hairs from Cheryl Thomas' apartment were found in the pantyhose mask. The answer was that they had been shaken from that mask.

The jury then returned to the jury room. When they asked for sandwiches to be sent in it was assumed that they would soon break off for the night, as there was such a huge amount of evidence and testimony to consider. However, at 9.20 pm they announced that they had reached a verdict.

'It's too soon,' said Louise Bundy. 'It's too soon.'

As the jury filed back into the courtroom, only the foreman Rudolph Treml glanced at Bundy. He handed seven slips of paper to Judge Cowart. After going through them, he handed them to the court clerk who read them out. Each one said: 'Guilty as charged.'

Throughout this process Bundy showed no emotion. He raised his eyebrows slightly and gently rubbed his chin with his right hand. When the final 'guilty' was read, sealing his fate, he sighed quietly. Three young women in the courtroom clapped their hands, while his mother cried.

Afterwards *The New York Times* described her thus: 'Louise Bundy is an intelligent and strong woman. The anguish of the last three years has left its mark, however, and she visibly sags when she is asked the hated little questions that she knows are designed to ferret out information that might explain her son to a world horrified by the acts for which he stands accused.'

But when questioned, she was adamant.

'All the psychiatric tests show he is not insane,' she told reporters. 'He was just a typical normal kid, a Boy Scout and a little bit above average in school. We have no explanation for why things happened as they did. Sooner or later, it will straighten out. Not a person who knew Ted well can believe he did it.'

Asked what Ted was told when he asked about his real father, she said he never asked her a question about that, not once.

Back home in Washington, Louise would lovingly show off Ted's picture, which stood in the living room with photographs of the brothers and sisters who continued to adore him despite the notoriety he had attracted. His brother Glen recalled how the family used to eat dinner together every night and attended Methodist church services every Sunday with the two younger children who hero-worshipped their oldest brother.

'We had such a good life going for us here,' Louise said. 'If anyone had ever hinted at anything like this happening in us, we'd all laugh. Now the only reason we're still holding our heads up is our faith. Our faith in God and Jesus Christ sustains us and always will. There's just no getting around it.'

Reporting reactions to the verdict, *The New York Times* described Carole Boone as 'a handsome woman in her early 30s' with a 'lithe body'. She had had a direct manner, which was attributed to her experience directing an office in state government.

'She, a sometime girlfriend, also loves Ted Bundy and has great faith in him,' the newspaper said.

'I'm an agnostic and I don't believe blindly in causes or people,' she said. 'I know Theodore well. I know how his mind works. His faults are not serious ones, but charming human qualities. He does have a temper, but it is not a violent one. So many of his good qualities have now been turned into evil ones because people think he is guilty. He's very bright, so now that has been turned into "evil genius". His wit has been turned into an act of cynicism by people repelled at the thought of a so-called "killer" having a sense of humour. If someone accepts his guilt, then every extraneous piece of information developed about him takes on a negative cast. He's very conscious of not wanting to vegetate, finding himself altered by prison life. He has already undergone a pretty shocking transformation from a Dan Evans Republican to being a fugitive.'

After being convicted Bundy was taken to the conference room, where he began to phone reporters.

'I just read them all wrong,' he told Richard Larsen of the *Seattle Times*, speaking of the jury. 'We thought we had some holdouts.'

James Bennett, the juror Bundy had been depending on, told the *Miami Herald* that he thought Bundy was 'incapable of emotion and he was convinced of Bundy's guilt by the bite mark evidence. It seemed crucial to the other members of the jury,' the newspaper reported.

'We wondered that if a guy made bite marks like that, wouldn't he take the trouble to alter his mouth?' Bennett said. 'I mean, I would have knocked out all my teeth before they caught me.'

The foreman of the jury, Rudolph Treml, a Texaco engineer, said he was even-handed to start with. Initially, he thought: 'Here was a guy in a Madison Avenue suit with his shoes shined and who looked just like me. I couldn't do such a horrible thing. How could he have?'

But as the trial went on, Treml changed his mind.

'There were some things that didn't quite piece together,' he said. 'Everything just kept on building. It couldn't be just so much coincidence.'

The jury was returned to the Sonesta Beach Hotel to await the opening of the penalty phase of the trial, which was scheduled to begin on Saturday 28 July, although the defence had asked for a further week's delay.

It was clear that prosecutors Simpson and McKeever were going to ask for the death penalty, so Bundy again asked for anti-capital punishment advocate Millard Farmer to represent him. But Judge Cowart said that he had already ruled on that.

'I consider the making of a motion a second time an effrontery to the court,' he said.

Next, Bundy asked for a Florida prison inmate to be called to testify that the law library in the prison system was woefully inadequate.

If given the chance to work there as a law clerk, he could upgrade the library, he said. Judge Cowart remarked that Bundy could have been a lawyer if he had not embarked on the path he had chosen in life.

Bundy entered another motion for a postponement.

'That falls on totally deaf ears,' said Judge Cowart.

Then Bundy said he wanted a plea bargain, as jury trials in capital cases were intrinsically unfair because a jury that returned a guilty verdict always opted for the death penalty. Judge Cowart pointed out that Bundy had been offered a plea bargain back in May and had turned it down. It was too late to go back on the decision after the event.

SENTENCING A MULTIPLE KILLER

Opening the penalty hearings, Carol DaRonch, now married, took the witness stand, but there was suddenly a huddle of the opposing attorneys. A word was whispered to the judge and she was asked to stand down. Instead, a negotiated statement from her would be read to the court.

Detective Jerry Thompson from Salt Lake City took the stand and produced a copy of Bundy's kidnapping conviction in Utah. Criminal Investigator Michael Fisher then showed that Bundy was supposed to have been in Colorado standing trial for murder at the time of the Chi Omega slayings. Reading a prepared statement to Bundy, he said: 'On January 15 1978, that you were under a sentence of imprisonment by the state of Utah and that you have not been paroled or otherwise released from that sentence.' As Bundy had not been 'paroled or otherwise released' the clear implication was that he had escaped.

Kathy Kleiner, who Bundy had beaten unconscious that night, told the court: 'I feel sorry for him. He needs help, but what he did, there's no way to compensate for that.'

Karen Chandler, who had also survived the attack, was less forgiving.

'Two people are dead because of him and I really think he should be too,' she said.

When Louise Bundy took the stand to plead for her son's life, she was naturally distressed.

'Settle down, mother,' said Judge Cowart. 'We haven't lost a mother in a long time, so just don't be nervous, okay.'

She explained that, along with Ted, she had four other children.

'We tried to be very conscientious parents, ones who did things with our children, gave them the best we could on a middle-class income,' she said. 'But, mostly we wanted to give them lots of love.'

Mrs Bundy then talked with pride about Ted's schooling, his teenage jobs, his dedication to Asian studies, his political activities and his jobs with the Seattle Crime Commission and the Governor Evans campaign.

'I've always had a very special relationship with all my children,' she said. 'We tried to keep them all equal, but Ted, being the oldest, you might say was my pride and joy. Our relationship was always very special. We'd talk a lot together, and his brothers and sisters thought of him as just the top person in their lives, as we all do.'

Then she was directed to the matter in hand.

'Have you considered the possibility that Ted might be executed?' Margaret Good asked.

'Yes, I've considered that possibility,' Mrs Bundy said. 'I had to because of the existence of such in this state. I consider the death penalty itself to be the most primitive, barbaric thing that one human can impose on another. And I've always felt that way. It has nothing to do with what's happened here. My Christian upbringing tells me that to take another's life under any circumstances is wrong, and I don't believe the state of Florida is above the laws of God. Ted can be very useful, in many ways, to many people, living. Gone from us would be like taking a part of all of us and throwing it away.'

'And if Ted were to be confined, to spend the rest of his life in prison?' Good asked.

'Oh,' his mother said. 'Of course, yes.'

Listening to his mother for the first time, Ted Bundy was moved to tears. Larry Simpson then made his concluding argument for the death penalty. 'The whole four to five weeks that we've been here in this courtroom has been for one reason. And that is because Theodore Robert Bundy took it upon himself to act as the judge, jury, and everybody else involved in this case and took the lives of Lisa Levy and Margaret Bowman,' he said. 'That is what this case has been all about. They can stand before you and ask for mercy. How nice it would have been if Lisa Levy's and Margaret Bowman's mothers could have been there that morning of January 15, 1978, and asked for mercy for them.'

Margaret Good argued that executing Ted Bundy would be to admit that he could not be healed. The death penalty should only be used in the case of a heinous crime. This was not one, she said. 'One of the factors of the definition is whether or not the victim suffered, whether there was torture or unnecessary cruelty to the victims. I believe you recall the testimony of Dr Wood where he stated explicitly that both of these women were rendered unconscious by a blow to the head. They were sleeping. They felt no pain. They didn't even know what was happening to them. It was not heinous, atrocious, or cruel because of the fact that they were not aware of impending death, they did not suffer, and there was no element of torture involved whatsoever to the victims who died.'

It was an appeal that, not unnaturally, fell on deaf ears. The jury withdrew for an hour and 40 minutes. They held three ballots. At one point, there was a deadlock – six for death and six against. The impasse was broken by ten minutes of 'prayer and meditation,' one juror said. One key factor in their decision was Bundy's callous cross-examination of Officer Crew. It was, a juror said, 'a mockery of our system.' In the end, they decided that Ted Bundy was to be electrocuted.

Judge Cowart still had the power to overturn the jury's decision, but he had already sentenced three murderers to the electric chair since the death penalty had been re-introduced. He borrowed directly from the wording of the statute re-imposing the death penalty in the state of Florida. 'This court finds that the killings were indeed heinous, atrocious and cruel in that they were extremely wicked, shockingly evil, vile and the product of a design to inflict a high degree of pain and with utter indifference to human life,' he said.

Bundy then got his chance to address the court.

'I'm not asking for mercy,' he said. 'For I find it somewhat absurd to ask for mercy for something I did not do. In a way, this is my opening statement. What we've seen here is just the first round, second round, early round of a long battle, and I haven't given up by any means. I believe if I'd been able to develop fully the evidence – which supports my innocence which indeed I think created a reasonable doubt – been able to have quality representation, I'm confident that I would have been acquitted, and, in the event I get a new trial, will be acquitted.

'It wasn't easy sitting through this trial for a number of reasons. But the main reason it was not easy in the early part of the case was the presentation of the state's case on what took place in the Chi Omega House, the blood, the pictures, the bloodstained sheets. And to note the state was trying to find me responsible was not easy. And it was not easy, nor did I ignore the families of these young women. I do not know them. And I do not think it's hypocritical of me, God knows, to say I sympathize with them, to the best I can. Nothing like this has ever happened to anyone close to me.

'But I'm telling the court, and I'm telling those people close to the victims in this case: I'm not the one responsible for the acts in the Chi Omega House or Dunwoody Street. And I'll tell the court I'm really not able to accept the verdict, because, although the verdict found in part that those crimes had been committed, they erred in finding who committed them.

'And as a consequence I cannot accept the sentence even though one will be imposed and even though I realize the lawful way the court will impose it – because it is not a sentence on me; it is a sentence on someone else who is not standing here today. So I will be tortured for and receive the pain for that act... but I will not share the burden or the guilt.'

Bundy then renewed his diatribe against the press.

'It is sad but true that the media thrives on sensation and they thrive on evil and they thrive on things taken out of context.'

Of course, Bundy also had to play up the importance of the drama being played out. 'And now the burden is on this court. And I don't envy you. The court is like a hydra right now. It's been asked to dispense no mercy as the maniac at the Chi Omega House dispensed no mercy. It's asked to consider this case as a man and a judge. And you're asked also to render the wisdom of a god. It's like some incredible Greek tragedy. It must have been written sometime and it must be one of those ancient Greek plays that portrays the three faces of man.'

Judge Cowart was unmoved.

'Mr Bundy,' he said. 'The court is going to sentence the person found guilty of the offense. Your name, sir, was in the verdict form. It is ordered that you be put to death by a current of electricity, that that current be passed through your body until you are dead.'

His duty done, Judge Cowart said softly: 'Take care of yourself, young man.'

'Thank you,' said Bundy.

'I say that to you sincerely; take care of yourself,' Judge Cowart continued. 'It's a tragedy for this court to see such a total waste of humanity that I've experienced in this courtroom. You're a bright young man. You'd have made a good lawyer, and I'd have loved to have you practice in front of me. But you went another way, partner. Take care of yourself. I don't have any animosity to you. I want you to know that.'

'Thank you.'

'Take care of yourself.'

'Thank you,' said Bundy, reconciled to his fate.

CHAPTER TWELVE
Death Row

TED BUNDY occupied a cell on Death Row in Florida State Prison two doors from 'Old Sparky', the electric chair. He was held in Q Wing, which also housed what Bundy called 'the uncontrollable and insane from all around the institution.' These included 'the infamous "shit-eater" whose grotesque fetish is closely followed by the "shit-buyer" who purchases the stuff from other inmates and smears it all over his body,' he wrote to Carole Boone. Bundy felt he did not belong with them.

At first other inmates assumed he was a rich college boy and tried to sell him watches, borrow money and steal things from him. His response was to try and build a reputation as a 'stand-up con'. He refused to take down posters his mother had sent him and spat at the guard who tried to make him do it. He got 30 days loss of privileges. Then another inmate called him a sissy.

A Raiford electric chair like the one used in Florida.

'I doubt that I can duplicate the string of red-hot expletives that came out of my mouth,' he told journalist and author Stephen G. Michaud. 'It was something like: "You dog mutherf***in' punk, bring your fat ass down here I'll show you who's a sissy. I'll turn you out you mutherf***er. I'll leave you on the floor dyin' in your own blood. I'll slit you right open, mutherf***er!" Or words to that effect.'

News spreading of the savage nature of his crimes also helped secure his standing. Other inmates became frightened of what he might do if pushed. Left alone, he had plenty of fan mail to occupy his time. Some argued that he had a nice face so he could not be a killer. Maybe he was a political prisoner!

Christian fundamentalists got in touch with him in an attempt to save his soul. Then there were the groupies. Some wanted to mother him, while others saw him as a fantasy lover. The most dedicated was a woman called Janet. Although she was married, she barraged him with passionate love letters and photographs, asking him to send pictures back. When he sent a single reply, it became an article of devotion.

'I kissed it all over and held it to me,' she wrote back. 'I don't mind telling you I am crying. I just don't see how I can stand it anymore. I love you so much, Ted.'

Janet was fiercely jealous of Carole Boone.

'You can't imagine how bad it hurts me and still is tearing my insides out,' she said.

When Janet turned up with the other groupies at the Kimberly Leach murder trial, which had been moved from

Lake City to Orlando in Orange County, Florida, Bundy wrote to Carole, asking her not to sit in the same row as Janet.

'When I look at you, there she sits contemplating me with her mad eyes like a deranged seagull studying a clam,' he said. 'I can feel her spreading hot sauce on me already.'

In his letters to Carole, Bundy also dismissed the Orlando trial as a 'non-event'. He took on a new attorney named J. Victor 'Vic' Africano. The public defender Milo I. Thomas had excused himself because he was a close friend of the Leach family. Africano had sat in on the Chi Omega trial in Miami and saw little chance of getting an acquittal. Bundy also conceded that he would probably be convicted again, protesting that the odds were stacked against him while repeatedly asserting: 'They just can't prove it.'

FACING JUSTICE FOR KIMBERLY LEACH'S MURDER

Again, Bundy wanted to go on the witness stand. Africano said he would only put him on the stand if Bundy would tell him, to his satisfaction, where he was every minute of the day between 3 February to 13 February 1978. Bundy consulted Carole over the matter and decided not to take the stand.

Africano considered an insanity plea – one where Bundy would not actually have to admit his guilt this time. It would be done on the basis of unrefuted psychiatric testimony at the Chi Omega trial to the effect that, if he had committed the attacks, he was insane. Africano consulted Dr Tanay, but he did not think that argument would hold water in court.

With the help of Lynn Thompson, on loan from public defender Mike Minerva's office in Tallahassee, and investigator Don Kennedy, who worked for the Lake City public defender, Africano set about trying to show that the prosecution's case could not be proved beyond reasonable doubt.

The prosecutor was Assistant State Attorney George R. 'Bob' Dekle, who had the appearance a 'good ol' boy'. He kept a chaw of tobacco in one cheek and boasted he could spit the juice 20 feet. This was misleading. He also read Homer in the original Greek, translated the Bible and quoted Shakespeare in his briefs.

Dekle was highly motivated. He had joined in the search for Kimberly Leach in Lake City and had recently become a father himself. Studying the other cases linked to Bundy, he drew up a chart making comparisons to the abduction and murder of Kimberly. This was disallowed on the grounds that it did not include the Chi Omega case, which was the only case where Bundy had been convicted and was glaringly dissimilar. Judge Wallace Jopling ruled that only the evidence concerning Leslie Parmenter would be allowed. She was of a similar age and had been approached the day before Kimberly went missing.

Again, the guarded confessions Bundy had made on the Chapman-Patchen-Bodiford tapes were disallowed. However, what Dekle had in his favour was that Bundy had name recognition of 98 per cent in Orange County – the same as the sitting president Jimmy Carter. He was so well known that a local DJ opened his morning show with the line: 'Watch out, girls. Ted Bundy's in town.'

Indeed, his notoriety had spread much further afield. A transvestite from Pennsylvania wearing a platinum wig turned up in court and slipped off his fake leopard-skin jacket to reveal a T-shirt saying 'Send Bundy to Iran' – the country was at that time embroiled in a revolution that would bring down its ruling Shah and usher in an Islamic state. While Bundy still had the support of his female fans, including Carole Boone, who had moved to Florida full time, his mother did not turn out this time.

Another thing in Dekle's favour was Bundy himself. He was no longer the slim handsome man he had been in court in Miami. He had put on 30 lb (14 kg) with a waistline bulging from his trousers, sagging jowls and sunken eyes. His behaviour did him no favours either.

'Would you please take this seriously,' he shouted at a court stenographer who had a smile on her face.

His demeanour was not helped by packed lunches that Carole prepared for him. These often contained vodka or Valium. In court his speech was slurred and once he barely made it back to his cell before passing out.

Over 130 prospective jurors were called in a panel selection that took two weeks. Almost everyone thought that Bundy was guilty already. However, State Attorney Jerry Blair of the state prosecutor's office pointed out that moving the venue again would be futile. There was nowhere in Florida where Bundy was not already infamous.

An all-white jury of five men and seven women was selected. The last panel member was Pat Walski, an employee of the *Orlando Sentinel Star*. He admitted that his impression of Bundy was negative, but he told Judge Jopling he could put that aside.

'Look what they are doing,' Bundy yelled at the judge. 'They want people who bring their prejudices to court and you're playing their game.'

Nevertheless, Africano said that he would accept the jury 'with reservations.' Again Bundy reacted badly.

'I'm not accepting it,' he said. 'I can't accept it.'

He was then moved to histrionics.

'I'm leaving,' Bundy said, attempting to stalk out of the courtroom. 'This is a game and I won't be a party to it! I'm not staying in this kind of Waterloo, you understand?'

Returning to the defence desk, he calmed down, only to explode again. This time he turned his wrath on Blair who, as Dekle's boss in the State Attorney's office, was technically head of the prosecution team. Bundy slammed his hand down on Judge Jopling's bench and yelled at Blair: 'Try to make me stay. You want a circus? I'll make a circus. I'll rain on your parade, Jack. You'll see a thunderstorm.'

He headed for the door again, his face contorted with rage. The bailiff blocked his path.

'Sit down, Mr Bundy,' ordered Judge Jopling.

'You know how far you can push me!' said Bundy.

'Sit down, Mr Bundy,' Judge Jopling said again.

Sloping back to the defence table once more, Bundy stage-whispered to Africano: 'It's no use. We've lost the jury. There's no point in playing the game.'

These outbursts caused enmity between the prosecution and defence teams, who refused to co-operate by sharing documents during the pre-trial 'discovery' process. In a session in the judge's chambers Dekle called Africano a 'self-righteous ass' for constantly referring to the death penalty as 'the final insult.' This drew a reprimand from Judge Jopling.

Dekle opened the prosecution case on 21 January. He called a 73-year-old crossing guard named Clinch Edenfield, who testified that he had seen Bundy in a white van near Lake City Junior High School on the morning Kimberly Leach went missing. However, under cross-examination by Lynn Thompson, Edenfield admitted that he had not identified Bundy until he had seen him on TV. During deposition, he had said that he knew he had picked the right man in a photo line-up because an FBI agent had winked at him. He also said that the morning was sunny, when it was windy and wet.

Lake City housewife Jacqueline Moore testified that she had seen a white van weaving down Highway 90. The driver's head was bobbing up and down in a way that suggested, the prosecution contended, that he was restraining a struggling victim. The van disappeared down a turn-off at Live Oak towards the place where Kimberly's body was found. But Moore had not recognized Bundy until she had seen one of his court outbursts on TV the previous Friday. Judge Jopling ruled that her testimony was inadmissible.

Then firefighter 'Andy' Andersen testified that he had seen a man who 'strongly resembled' Bundy leading a distraught-looking girl to a white van parked outside Lake City Junior High

School. But again, he had only come forward after seeing Bundy on TV six months after the event. He had then undergone two sessions of hypnosis to improve his recall. Vic Africano maintained that he had been unduly influenced by the hypnotists. Another flaw in his testimony was that if the van had been parked where he said he saw it, it would have caused a traffic jam during the morning rush hour.

John Farhat, the owner of the Green Acres Sporting Goods store in Jacksonville, was shown a picture of two price tags from his shop that had been found in the Florida State University's media centre van. One said '$24'; the other, stuck on top of it, said '$26'. Farhat testified that the only item in his shop that had gone up from $24 to $26 was a Buck hunting knife with a ten-inch (25 cm) blade. However, in a photo line-up he had picked out a garage mechanic from Live Oak as the man who had bought the knife. In court, he identified Bundy.

'That's a damn lie,' yelled Bundy.

While the attorneys conferred with the judge over the defendant's outburst, Bundy calmed down. But that night on the phone he told Carole: 'I told Vic I'm coming unglued. I just can't keep it together anymore. I'm sorry. I'm just starting to lose it. I was strong as long as I can be. I don't know what these guys expect of me. Not only to just go through jury selection and listen to all that rot, but then listening to witness after witness after witness. Lie! Lie! Lie! Lie! I'm fed up with it! I need some goddamn special attention. I demand it.'

Dekle then called Dr Lipkovic, who had performed the post-mortem. He testified that, in his opinion, Kimberly had died from 'homicidal violence to the neck region.' The jury were shown slides of the hog shed where Kimberly had been found, with the body still in place. In the darkened courtroom, Bundy grew visibly aroused.

While the serology on the semen found on Cheryl Thomas' sheets had proved inconclusive, this time the forensic work proved a clincher. Underpants found next to Kimberly's body carried semen from an O blood-type secretor such as Bundy. Blood on the seat of Kimberly's jeans found in the back of the white media van was of type B – Kimberly's blood type – and contained a specific blood protein known to be in her blood. This indicated that she had been stripped, raped, re-clothed, then stripped again.

Dekle established that the FSU media centre van had been missing from 5 February until 13 February. Credit card slips demonstrated that Bundy had been in Jacksonville the day Leslie Parmenter had been approached and in Lake City the day Kimberly Leach went missing. Leon County Deputy Keith Dawes testified that he had seen Bundy in a stolen green Toyota with Florida licence plate number 13D-11300 in Tallahassee. That same number Danny Parmenter had reported was on the white van whose driver had approached his little sister Leslie in Jacksonville.

Mary Lynn Hinson, a microanalyst at the Florida Department of Law Enforcement's laboratory, testified that fibres from the interior of the white media van matched those found on the clothing of both Bundy and Kimberly Leach, indicating it was 'very probable they were in physical contact.' Although the 'very 'probable' gave some room for the defence to contest Hinson's testimony, there were so many cross-comparisons that they could find no expert witness willing to challenge them.

The defence depended on the testimony of Atlanta Medical Examiner Doctor Joseph Burton, who said that the decomposition of Kimberly's corpse meant that the cause of death could not positively be determined. This backfired when he continued: 'While my study of findings could not rule out accidental, suicidal or natural causes, all three are way down my list.'

The jury took seven and a half hours to convict. Africano, who had been betting on three, said: 'The one thing I like about that is that at least there is no suspense.'

In his final speech Bundy broke down in tears. Meanwhile, Carole applied for a marriage licence. However, Orange County Jail refused permission for the couple to marry on the grounds that marriage was 'not in the inmate's best interest'. Bundy was willing to let it go at that. After all, he was already under two death sentences and was expecting another one shortly.

MARRIED IN A MATTER OF SECONDS

Under Florida state law it was necessary to have blood tests before being allowed to marry. Again, the prison authorities prevented a doctor from taking Bundy's blood, but he successfully argued to Judge Jopling that he had a right to see a doctor.

Carole could not find a minister who would perform the ceremony, but she researched the matter and found that a public declaration in an open courtroom in the presence of court officials was enough to make a marriage legal.

The penalty hearing was set for 9 February 1980, two years to the day since Kimberly Leach had gone missing. Bundy would act as his own attorney and would call Carole as a character witness. For the event, he wore a blue polka-dot bow tie, a blue sports jacket, khaki slacks and Argyle socks. She wore black – a skirt and knitted sweater over a white open-neck blouse.

In front of hundreds of witnesses – the judge, jurors, attorneys and spectators – Bundy would lead her through the required questions.

'Where do you reside?' Bundy asked.

'I am a permanent resident of Seattle, Washington,' she replied.

'Could you explain when you met me, how long you have known me... our relationship?' he said.

Carole recalled their meeting at the Department of Emergency Services office in Olympia and talked of the closeness that had developed between them as Ted's legal problems grew.

'Several years ago, our relationship evolved into a more serious, romantic sort of thing,' she said.

'Is it serious?' Bundy asked.

'Serious enough that I want to marry him,' she told the jury.

'Can you tell the jury if you've ever observed any violent or destructive tendencies in my character or personality?'

'I've never seen anything in Ted that indicates any destructiveness toward any other people, and we have been associated with Ted in virtually every circumstance. He's been involved with my family. I've never seen anything in Ted that indicates any kind of destructiveness, any kind of hostility. He's a warm, kind, patient man,' she said.

Over the prosecution's objections, Carole stated that she felt it was not right for an individual or the state to take the life of a human being.

'Ted is a large part of my life,' she told the jury. 'He is vital to me.'

'Do you want to marry me?' Bundy asked.

'Yes,' she answered.

'I do want to marry you,' Ted said.

Prosecutors Dekle and Blair objected. Bundy turned to his attorneys, who told him he had almost blown it by using the wrong terminology. Marriage was a contract, not just an intention or promise. He would have one more chance on redirect, following cross-examination, to get the wording right.

State Attorney Blair questioned Carole, suggesting that there might be financial reasons she wanted to marry Bundy. She denied this. He questioned the timing of the proposal, coming as it did just as the jury was deliberating the death penalty. Again, Carole did not rise to this. Meanwhile, Bundy conferred frantically with his lawyers.

When Bundy rose to question Carole on redirect, he knew what he must say to make the marriage valid.

'Will you marry me?' he asked her.

'Yes,' she replied.

'Then I do hereby marry you.'

It was done so quickly the prosecution had no chance to stop it. Ted Bundy and Carole Boone were now man and wife.

Blair decried the courtroom marriage as 'a little Valentine's Day charade.' Derision was hardly necessary. The jury were unmoved by the proceedings. Bundy concluded with a rambling plea for his life that lasted 40 minutes.

The jury then retired. Returning after 45 minutes' deliberation, they decided that Ted Bundy was to die. Bundy jumped to his feet and shouted at Judge Jopling: 'Tell the jury they were wrong!'

On 12 February Judge Jopling also adopted the language of Florida state law concerning execution. Bundy, he said, had been convicted once again of a crime that was 'extremely wicked, shockingly evil and vile.' He was sentenced for a third time to be electrocuted, for the murder of Kimberly Leach.

As Bundy stood to receive his sentence, he had in his hand a red envelope. It was a St Valentine's card for his new bride. Within an hour Bundy was in a helicopter, lifting off from the courthouse roof and taking him back to Florida State Prison where he would await the sentence to be carried out. There would, of course, be numerous appeals before he finally went to the electric chair, nine years later.

CHAPTER THIRTEEN
Fresh Confessions

TED BUNDY was acclimatized to living on Death Row. His disruptive behaviour in the courtroom earned him the respect of the other prisoners. The black inmates allowed him to play basketball with them once a week.

Carole and her son Jamey visited once a week. They met in an open room. Touching was allowed and although they were under the eyes of armed guards, sometimes it was possible to have sex behind the water cooler or in the toilet. As a result Carole bore Bundy a child, who they named Rosa.

Carole also smuggled dope into the prison in her vagina. At their meetings Bundy clandestinely transferred it to his rectum. This worked well enough when she used smooth, round containers she bought at the chemist's, but one time she resorted to aspirin bottles, which it took Bundy two days to remove.

Three weeks after the end of the Kimberly Leach trial, Stephen G. Michaud and Hugh Aynesworth began interviewing Bundy for their book *The Only Living Witness: The True Story of Serial Sex Killer Ted Bundy*. Michaud would befriend Bundy and chat casually to him, while Aynesworth would research the cases and confront Bundy with hard evidence. They also interviewed Carole, who continued to maintain that her new husband could not be guilty and came up with a list of alternative suspects, which Aynesworth soon discounted.

Bundy did not expect them to believe he was innocent. While Carole insisted that proof of his innocence could be found, Bundy was stoic, saying: 'The facts to prove unequivocally that I'm innocent are not there.'

Nevertheless, he pledged his full co-operation, while continuing to be evasive under questioning. Their conversations led Michaud to believe that, inside, Bundy was still a little boy – the emotionally twisted one who left butcher's knives in his Aunt Julie's bed.

'It was then that I chanced the offer for this child to "speculate" on what had happened,' Michaud said.

Bundy accepted this offer and talked about what had happened in the third person. Michaud and Aynesworth took the tapes of these conversations to Doctor Al Carlisle, who had interviewed Bundy at Utah State Prison. He concurred with their theory. As a boy Bundy had been hurt by girls and felt inferior. He wanted to have a relationship with a girl, but felt he would not be accepted. Dr Carlisle also said that Bundy was more intelligent than most killers. He was cold and could compartmentalize as if he were an actor playing a role on stage.

Other sex killers liked their victims conscious and alive, so they could enjoy the feeling of being in control. Bundy liked his victims inert – either unconscious or dead. Again, Dr Carlisle found this 'childlike'. However, like other sex killers Bundy depersonalized his victims, finding planning his crimes and the hunting of his prey exciting. This made him feel better, smarter and more powerful than his quarry.

Aynesworth began confronting Bundy with the details of his crimes, forcing him to admit that his way of achieving sexual gratification was abnormal. As Bundy still held on to the hope that he could avoid the electric chair, Aynesworth floated the possibility that he might save himself by confessing to all his crimes and revealing where the bodies as yet undiscovered had been left, then subjecting himself honestly to the probing of academic psychologists interested in his case. Bundy grew angry at this suggestion, denying that he had ever raised the possibility of escaping execution – only to be proved wrong when Aynesworth played back the tapes.

As the date of his execution drew near Bundy crumpled under the strain and said he wanted to end the interviews. He claimed to have studied Oriental philosophy that allowed him to live in the here and now, unconcerned with what had happened in the past and what was going to happen in the future. More disturbingly, he said he was now free of guilt.

'What's one less person on the face of the earth, anyway?' he said callously.

The election of conservative Ronald Reagan as president in 1980, after defeating liberal incumbent president Jimmy Carter, convinced Bundy that he was more certain than ever to die. But still he denied hurting anyone.

Bundy spent nine and a half years on Death Row, eluding three death warrants signed by Florida Governor Bob Graham, who went on to become a US Senator and ran for the Democratic presidential nomination in 2004. One of the warrants – for the murder of Kimberly Leach – was stayed with just six hours to go. Bundy had already been fitted for a funeral suit.

The New York chapter of vigilante group the Guardian Angels travelled to Florida to demonstrate against the stay of execution outside the jail, while motorists across the Sunshine State protested the new seatbelt law with bumper stickers that read: 'I'll buckle up when Bundy does. It's the law.'

When Bundy faced the first death warrant – for the Chi Omega killings – in February 1986, Polly Nelson and James Coleman of the prestigious Washington D.C. firm of Wilmer, Cutler & Pickering took on his case on a *pro bono* basis, and won him his first stay of execution from the US Supreme Court.

As they continued to fight off his death sentences, they tried to persuade Bundy that his only chance of avoiding execution was, again, entering an insanity plea. But, as before, Bundy insisted that he was entirely sane. Meanwhile, he found himself back in the limelight when NBC ran the made-for-TV movie *The Deliberate Stranger*, which purported to tell Bundy's story.

While Bundy would not discuss the Chi Omega murders with Nelson and Coleman, he was persuaded to give what they believed were the full list of his predations. Nelson was appalled, while what struck Coleman was Bundy's seeming indifference to what he had done. Without an insanity plea, they sought to show that Bundy had not been competent to stand trial in Florida and called in the psychiatrist and specialist in violence, Dr Dorothy Otnow Lewis. As well as interviewing him four times, she also spoke to family members and studied his medical records and court transcripts. Her diagnosis was that he was bipolar.

Nelson and Coleman won a new competency hearing in the Kimberly Leach case in Orlando in December 1987, where Dr Lewis presented her findings. She was convinced that the source of Bundy's problem was his grandfather. While there was no evidence that Samuel Cowell had abused his grandson or his daughter Louise, Dr Lewis testified that 'the family seemed to feel that it was very important for Mr Bundy, and for his mother, to get out of that household. To quote [Ted's great aunt] Ginny: "We felt Louise had to be rescued."'

This account of Bundy's childhood was diametrically opposed to the picture of a happy childhood he painted for others. Dr Lewis also speculated about the exact nature of the relationship between Samuel Cowell and his daughter. As for Bundy's father, was there ever a putative 'Jack Worthington', she asked? Dr Lewis also discovered that there was mental instability in the family. Louise's mother Eleanor had been hospitalized for psychotic depression and had been given electroshock therapy.

Michaud and Aynesworth also took their tapes to Doctor Louis Jolyon West, Director of the Neuropsychiatric Institute at UCLA, who was an expert on abused children. He concluded:

Bundy's best weird smile – Dr Lewis had discovered there had been a case of psychotic depression in the family, his mother's mother.

'Somewhere in that man's boyhood, a woman beat him with a stick.'

The tapes were subpoenaed by Florida's Deputy Attorney General. Nevertheless, US District Judge G. Kendall Sharp found that Bundy had been competent to stand trial, saying: 'It's not really competence on trial here. It's the death penalty. Everybody knows that.'

In 1984 Bundy contacted Bob Keppel, who was then working with the task force set up to catch the Green River Killer, who killed 49 women, dumping their bodies in King County, Washington State. The first five were found along the Green River. Like Bundy, this killer often returned to the bodies of his victims to have sex with them again.

Bundy offered his insight into the workings of a serial killer. Keppel visited Bundy in jail that November and recounted his interviews in *The Riverman: Ted Bundy and I Hunt for the Green River Killer*. Bundy shared what he had learned from his own career, from the literature he had studied and fellow killers on Death Row. He called the Green River Killer 'Riverman' and was plainly jealous of his success.

Keppel was also interested in clearing up other murders that Bundy may have committed. Bundy was clearly excited when Keppel showed him a photograph of the remains of a girl he suspected Bundy of killing in 1974 and was disappointed when Keppel brought no more crime scene pictures on subsequent visits.

Bundy also spent time with Special Agent Bill Hagmaier of the FBI's Behavioral Science Unit at the Bureau's academy in Quantico – now commonly known as the 'Hannibal Lecter Squad'.

He hinted that his victims numbered 30, not the hundreds that were being attributed to him.

Special Agent Hagmaier asked about Melissa Smith's make-up and Laura Aime's freshly washed hair. Bundy said: 'If you've got time, they can be anything you want them to be.'

He also admitted to taking Polaroid pictures of his victims as a souvenir, explaining: 'When you work hard to do something right, you don't want to forget it.'

He told Special Agent Hagmaier that the murders were not about lust or violence, but possession.

'They are part of you,' Bundy said. 'After a while, when you plan these, that person becomes a part of you and you are forever one.... Even after 20 or 30 it's the same thing because you are the last one there. You feel the last bit of breath leaving their body. You're looking into their eyes and, basically, a person in that situation is God. You then possess them and they shall forever be part of you. And the grounds where you kill them or leave them become sacred to you, and you will always be drawn back to them.'

The date of Bundy's execution was set yet again for 24 January 1989. On 16 January the warrant was drawn up to be signed by Governor Bob Martinez, who had succeeded Bob Graham. The following day, in the hope of buying time, Bundy said he was finally ready to talk.

On 18 January Jim Coleman began a last-ditch attempt to save Bundy's life in the state courts. He advised Bundy against trying to trade information for time, as this was an implicit admission of murder. Governor Martinez also ruled out any deal, saying: 'For him to be negotiating for his life over the bodies of others is despicable.'

Coleman's motion for a further stay of execution was denied in the state court on 19 January and moved on to the Florida Supreme Court. That day Jamey Boone visited the prison where Bundy, for the first time, openly admitted he was a murderer. Jamey begged him not to stage the press conference he planned to publicize his confession, on the grounds that his mother Louise had been hurt enough. She would not visit again.

On 20 January the Florida Supreme Court took just 50 minutes to throw out Coleman's motion. An appeal was scheduled for 9 am the following morning.

Special Agent Hagmaier visited Bundy again. Through the glass partition that now separated them, he said: 'This is it, isn't it?'

Bundy answered: 'I don't know, but I think it might be.'

Keppel also visited. Bundy described the murder of Georgann Hawkins to him and confirmed that she was the unidentified third victim lying on the Issaquah hillside alongside Janice Ott and Denise Naslund. He admitted that the bodies discovered on Taylor Mountain were his victims. He also admitted killing Donna Manson and three more victims in Washington who he did not identify, bringing the number he had killed in that state to 11 in all.

Bundy then grew upset that Keppel did not ask him why he had killed those women.

'I told him I wasn't interested in why,' said Keppel, 'that "why" never caught anybody. And he took a little offense at that. He said: "I'm sure you're interested when you go to crime scenes. It helps you understand this person a little bit more." I said: "No, we're interested in who and what, where and when and how."'

Bundy then burst into tears at the thought of going to the electric chair and said that he hoped the authorities would give him a bit more time if he cleared up the rest of the murders. He wanted another 60 or 90 days and asked for Keppel's help.

The following day Coleman's appeal was denied and news of Bundy's fresh confessions leaked to the news media. As Coleman predicted, the belated confessions undermined Bundy's argument that he had not been given a fair trial.

'Once Ted confessed to 11 murders, a judge could say: "Well, what difference does it make?"' Coleman said. But Bundy persisted in trying to cut a deal through another attorney named Diana Weiner. She approached Andrea Hillyer, Governor Martinez's Special Liaison Assistant with the Florida Department of Corrections, to convey Bundy's offer that he would resolve all the outstanding cases in exchange for a temporary reprieve. Meanwhile, Weiner was besieged by detectives from around the country trying to make appointments to interview her client.

Bundy met Colorado criminal investigator Michael Fisher and admitted the murder of Julie Cunningham, but would not discuss the murders of Denise Oliverson and Caryn Campbell. The following day he made a summary confession to killing Caryn, but Denise was not mentioned.

He also admitted to murders in Idaho, and told Dennis Couch, a detective from Salt Lake County Sheriff's Office, that he had killed Nancy Wilcox and Debra Kent. Detective Couch ran out of time before he could discuss Melissa Smith and Laura Aime. However, speaking with Special Agent Hagmaier, Bundy admitted those two murders as well.

Special Agent Hagmaier compiled a list: 11 victims in Washington State, including Kathy Parks and three victims who were unidentified; eight in Utah including three unidentified; three in Colorado; three in Florida; two in Oregon, both unidentified; two in Idaho, one of whom was unidentified; and one in California, again unidentified. There were 30 girls and young women in all.

Bundy denied rumours that he had killed women in New Jersey, Vermont and elsewhere in the north east. FBI agent Hagmaier also asked about 8-year-old Ann Burr, who disappeared in Tacoma, Washington, in August 1961. Again, Bundy denied having anything to do with it. However, he did admit decapitating at least 12 of his victims, saying he had burned Donna Manson's skull in Liz Kendall's fireplace. He kept another five heads in his room in the Rogers house.

Bundy's attorney Polly Nelson and Dr Lewis visited. Bundy said: 'I don't know why everyone is out to get me.'

'He really and truly did not have a sense of what he had done,' Dr Lewis said. Then, she said, they hugged and exchanged kisses.

'And that is how I became the last woman to kiss Ted Bundy,' she recalled in her book *Guilty by Reason of Insanity*. Polly Nelson left in tears.

Michael Fisher and other investigators visited Bundy again, but got little more out of him. He recorded a final interview on camera that would not be shown until the next day, after he was dead. A tearful Bundy said he didn't want to die and blamed pornography for his plight.

'Those of us who are, or who have been, so much influenced by violence in the media, in particular pornographic violence, are not some kind of inherent monsters,' Bundy said. 'We are your sons and we are your husbands and we grew up in regular families. And pornography can reach out and snatch a kid out of any house today. It snatched me out of my house 20, 30 years ago, as dedicated as my parents were – and they were diligent in protecting their children. And as good a Christian home as we had… and we had a wonderful Christian home, there is no protection against the kind of influences that are loose in society.'

The day before the execution, Andrea Hillyer arrived with three psychiatrists who would testify to Bundy's sanity in case Coleman managed to force another hearing on the matter. With just 14 hours to go, Bundy begged Hillyer for one last visit from Diane Weiner. Permission was denied. Coleman was also denied a last visit.

Bundy then drew up his will. Weiner was to have custody of his property, which included his credit of $709.66 at the prison canteen and his wedding ring.

He asked to be cremated and asked Weiner to scatter his ashes over the Cascade Mountains. This caused outrage in Seattle and Tacoma.

Bundy, his stepson Jamey and Jack Tanner, a friend who had arranged the last video interview, celebrated communion as best they could with crackers and cola. Hillyer checked with the US Supreme Court, only to find that Coleman's final three appeals points had been denied. Coleman and Nelson phoned Bundy to give him the bad news. He was visibly shaken.

In the early hours of 24 January 1989 Reverend Fred Lawrence, a Methodist minister from Gainesville, Florida, arrived. He sat outside Bundy's cell and they talked for the rest of the night. Bundy made no attempt to contact Carole, who had disappeared with their baby after learning of her husband's confessions. Bundy began to write her a last letter, but it was left unfinished.

He made a ten-minute call to his mother. She told him: 'We're all praying for you.' Her last words to him were: 'You will always be my precious son.' She also called Bundy the 'light of our lives.' He said God's spirit was with him.

When the call was over, she told a reporter from the *Tacoma News Tribune*: 'He sounds wonderful. He sounds very much at peace with himself. He said: "I'm so sorry I've given you all such grief, but a part of me was hidden all the time." And then he said: "But the Ted Bundy you knew also existed."'

Bundy did not order a last meal, so was given the traditional final fare: steak cooked medium-rare, eggs over easy, hash browns, toast with butter and jelly, milk and juice. He declined to eat it and drank a glass of water instead.

At around 6 am prison officers shaved Bundy's head and right calf where the electrode was to be attached. He then showered and conductive gel was applied to the shaved areas.

Prison Superintendent Jim Barton arrived with a tape recorder and asked Bundy if he had any final statement to make. He said he had and gave details of the murder of Denise Oliverson, saying he dumped her body in the river just west of Grand Junction, Colorado. He then admitted abducting 15-year-old Susan Curtis from the campus of Brigham Young University in June 1975. Smoking a last cigarette, Bundy again denied killing anyone in Vermont, New Jersey, Illinois, Texas or Miami.

At 6.57 am two prison guards escorted him to the execution chamber. Revd Lawrence and Jim Coleman were there. They exchanged nods. Bundy also exchanged nods with Jerry Blair, the Lake City State Attorney.

Demonstrators rejoice as Bundy is executed in Florida's electric chair.

A white hearse leaves Florida State Prison carrying away the body of Ted Bundy.

As Bundy was strapped into the electric chair, he addressed his last remarks to Coleman and Lawrence.

'Jim and Fred,' he said. 'I'd like you to give my love to my family and friends.'

His face was then covered.

The hooded executioner was thought to be a woman. At 7.06 am the superintendent signalled the go-ahead. She pressed the button and 2,000 volts surged though Bundy's body. His fists clenched. After a minute the power was turned off. At 7.10 am a paramedic felt for a pulse and found none.

Then at 7.16 am prison physician Doctor Frank Kilgo pulled back Bundy's leather hood and checked for movement of his pupils with a small torch. He then pronounced 42-year-old Ted Bundy dead.

Index